AL RIES is one of the w........ strategists. He is the co-author of such best-selling books as *Positioning: The Battle for Your Mind, Marketing Warfare* and *The 22 Immutable Laws of Marketing,* and the author of *Focus: The Future of Your Company Depends on It.*

LAURA RIES is a graduate of Northwestern University and a partner in the marketing strategy firm Ries & Ries, from which the authors do speaking engagements, write articles and act as consultants to major corporations, including Alcoa, Frito-Lay, Glaxo Wellcome, Merck and Pillsbury. Ries & Ries can be visited on the Web at www.ries.com.

THE
22
Immutable
Laws of
BRANDING

AL RIES and LAURA RIES

HarperCollinsBusiness
An Imprint of HarperCollinsPublishers

HarperCollinsBusiness
an imprint of HarperCollins*Publishers*
77–85 Fulham Palace Road,
Hammersmith, London W6 8JB

www.harpercollinsbusiness.com

This paperback edition 2000
1 3 5 7 9 8 6 4 2

First published in Great Britain by
HarperCollins*Publishers* 1999

First published in the United States by
HarperCollins Publishers 1998

ISBN 0 00 653129 622

Set in New Caledonia

Printed and bound in Great Britain by
Caledonian International Book Manufacturing Ltd, Glasgow

Dedicated to Mary Lou,
a wife, a mother, and a friend

Contents

Introduction

Our last book, *Focus: The Future of Your Company Depends on It,* described ways that companies could focus themselves to become more profitable and more powerful. This book applies the concept of focus to the marketing process itself.

Marketing has become too complicated, too confusing, and too full of jargon. In most companies, marketing work is done by many different functional groups. Advertising, product development, product design, consumer research, sales promotion, and public relations, to name a few.

Coordinating and integrating these functional groups has become a major activity of its own. If marketing is to fulfill its promise as the driving force in an organization, the marketing process itself has to be simplified. In other words, focused.

What is the single most important objective of the marketing process? What is the glue that holds the broad range of marketing functions together?

We believe it's the process of branding.

Marketing is building a brand in the mind of the prospect. If you can build a powerful brand, you will have a powerful marketing program. If you can't, then all the advertising, fancy packaging, sales promotion, and public relations in the world won't help you achieve your objective.

Marketing is branding. The two concepts are so inextricably linked that it is impossible to separate them. Furthermore, since everything a company does can contribute to the brand-building process, marketing is not a function that can be considered in isolation.

Marketing is what a company is in business to do. Marketing is a company's ultimate objective. That's why everyone who works in a corporation should be concerned with marketing and, specifically, with the laws of branding.

If the entire company is the marketing department, then the entire company is the branding department.

As illogical as it might seem, we can visualize a time when the marketing concept itself will become obsolete, to be replaced by a new concept called "branding."

What is accelerating this trend is the decline of selling. As a profession and as a function, selling is slowly sinking like the *Titanic*. Today most products and services are bought, not sold. And branding greatly facilitates this process. Branding "pre-sells" the product or service to the user. Branding is simply a more efficient way to sell things.

That old expression "Nothing happens until somebody sells something" is being replaced by today's slogan: "Nothing happens until somebody brands something."

Take a supermarket or drugstore with brands lining the shelves. A lot of buying takes place as customers pick and choose between various brands. But where's the selling?

The selling is in the brand. In this age of multimedia, the verbal endorsement of a product, essentially its guarantee, is represented by the brand name, rather than by the personal recommendation of a salesperson.

What has been true for years in the supermarket is now beginning to catch on across the marketing landscape. Take the mecca of high-pressure salesmanship, the used-car lot. Today the fast-talking used-car salesman is being replaced by brand-name lots AutoNation USA and Car-Max. In a low-key environment with literally thousands of cars to choose from, shoppers decide which one to buy with a minimum amount of help from salaried representatives patrolling the lot.

In concept, the used-car lot, once the pinnacle of finagling, is becoming more like a Wal-Mart supercenter. Products are stocked in depth, artfully arranged and reasonably priced, but are never "sold."

The ultimate in brand-centered buying is on the Internet. Consumers are purchasing cars from Web sites without ever seeing the cars or going for a test drive.

What's happening in the automobile industry is also

happening in many other fields. In financial services, for example, companies like Charles Schwab, E*Trade, Fidelity, and Vanguard are brands that offer direct access, cheaper commissions, and on-line customer service, giving traditional stockbrokers a run for their money.

There's a seismic shift taking place in the world of business. The shift from selling to buying. This shift is enhanced, accelerated, and caused by the rise of brands.

What Is a Brand?

The essence of the marketing process is building a brand in the minds of consumers. But what, you may ask, is a brand?

Some managers believe that brands possess unique identities and qualities separate from their company or product names. "They made their name into a brand," said one analyst about a company's successful marketing program.

They made their name into a brand. What does this statement mean? In truth, nothing. In the consumer's mind, there is no difference between a company or product name and a brand name.

Obviously, marketing people have all sorts of definitions for company names, division names, brand names, and model names; not to mention subbrands, megabrands, flanker brands, and other esoteric variations of the branding process.

When you look inside the mind of the prospect, how-ever, all of these variations disappear. Imagine a customer saying to a friend, "What do you think of this new flanker brand?"

"Not much. I stick with megabrands or subbrands."

People don't talk that way. Nor do they think that way. To paraphrase Gertrude Stein, "A brand is a brand is a brand."

A brand name is nothing more than a word in the mind, albeit a special kind of word. A brand name is a noun, a proper noun, which like all proper nouns is usually spelled with a capital letter.

Any and every proper noun is a brand whether or not it's owned by an individual, a corporation, or a community. Patagonia is a brand name for a clothing line, but it's also a brand name for the tourist industries of Argentina and Chile interested in promoting travel to this pristine and beautiful place. Philadelphia is a brand name for the lead-ing cream cheese, but it's also a brand name for the city of brotherly love.

Brands are not limited to the 1,200,000 trademarks reg-istered with the U.S. government. Nor the additional mil-lions of names and logotypes registered with other countries around the world.

Any proper noun is a brand. You are a brand. (And if you want to be truly successful in life, you should consider yourself a brand and act accordingly.)

The power of a brand lies in its ability to influence purchasing behavior. But a brand name on a package is not the same thing as a brand name in a mind.

The customer who stops at a 7-Eleven to pick up a loaf of bread and a quart of milk usually ends up purchasing two branded products. Yet there might be little or no brand preference in the buyer's mind. It's just a quart of milk and a loaf of bread.

Yet the same customer might also buy a six-pack of beer and a carton of cigarettes. Chances are high that the customer will search out a particular brand of beer and a particular brand of cigarettes to buy.

Conventional wisdom suggests that beer and cigarettes are different from bread and milk. Beer and cigarettes are brand buys. Bread and milk are commodity purchases.

While this may be literally true, it overlooks an important consideration. You can build a brand in any category, including bread and milk, as long as you follow the laws of branding. Some companies already have done so with brands like Lactaid (in milk) and Earth Grains (in bread).

If there ever was a commodity category, it's H_2O, otherwise known as water. Since almost every person in America has access to good, clean water out of the tap, there is no need to buy water from a store, but many people do.

Evian is such a powerful brand that the last time we bought 1.5 liters, we paid $1.69. That same day, on a per-liter basis, Evian was selling for 20 percent more than Budweiser, 40 percent more than Borden's milk, and 80 percent more than Coca-Cola. That's the power of branding.

What this book will do is to help you apply brand thinking or the "branding" process to your business. In other words, to turn your water into Evian. Or yourself into the next Bill Gates.

Aim high. You can never achieve more than you aspire to.

What Is Branding?

From a business point of view, branding in the marketplace is very similar to branding on the ranch.

A branding program should be designed to differentiate your cow from all the other cattle on the range. Even if all the cattle on the range look pretty much alike.

A successful branding program is based on the concept of singularity. It creates in the mind of the prospect the perception that there is no product on the market quite like your product.

Can a successful brand appeal to everybody? No. The same concept of singularity makes certain that no one brand can possibly have a universal appeal.

Yet, broadening the base, widening the appeal, and extending the line are all popular trends in marketing. The same forces that try to increase a company's market share are the forces that undermine the power of the brand.

How to direct and control those forces, both inside and outside of the corporation, is one of the major themes of this book.

Chevrolet used to be the largest-selling automobile brand in America. In 1986, for example, the Chevrolet division of General Motors sold 1,718,839 cars. But trying to be all things to everyone undermined the power of the brand. Today Chevrolet sells less than a million cars per year and has fallen to second place in the market behind Ford.

1

The Law of Expansion

*The power of a brand is inversely
proportional to its scope.*

Think Chevrolet. What immediately comes to mind?

Having trouble? It's understandable.

Chevrolet is a large, small, cheap, expensive car . . . or
truck.

When you put your brand name on everything, that
name loses its power. Chevrolet used to be the best-selling automobile brand in America. No longer. Today Ford
is the leader.

Think Ford. Same problem. Ford and Chevrolet, once
very powerful brands, are burning out. Slowly heading for
the scrap heap.

Ford buyers talk about their Tauruses. Or their Bron-
cos. Or their Explorers. Or their Escorts.

Chevrolet buyers talk about their ... Well, what do Chevy buyers talk about? Except for the Corvette, there are no strong brands in the rest of the Chevrolet car line. Hence, Chevy's brand-image problem.

Chevrolet has ten separate car models. Ford has eight. That's one reason Ford outsells Chevrolet. The power of a brand is inversely proportional to its scope.

Why does Chevrolet market all those models? Because it wants to sell more cars. And in the short term, it does. But in the long term, it undermines its brand name in the mind of the consumer.

Short term versus long term. Do you broaden the line in order to increase sales in the short term? Or do you keep a narrow line in order to build the brand in the mind and increase sales in the future?

Do you build the brand today in order to move merchandise tomorrow? Or do you expand the brand today in order to move the goods today and see it decline tomorrow?

The emphasis in most companies is on the short term. Line extension, megabranding, variable pricing, and a host of other sophisticated marketing techniques are being used to milk brands rather than build them. While milking may bring in easy money in the short term, in the long term it wears down the brand until it no longer stands for anything.

What Chevrolet did with automobiles, American Express is doing with credit cards. AmEx used to be the premier, prestige credit card. Membership had its privileges. Then it started to broaden its product line with new cards and services, presumably to increase its market share. AmEx's goal was to become a financial supermarket.

In 1988, for example, American Express had a handful of cards and 27 percent of the market. Then it started to introduce a blizzard of new cards including: Senior, Student, Membership Miles, Optima, Optima Rewards Plus Gold, Delta SkyMiles Optima, Optima True Grace, Optima Golf, Purchasing, and Corporate Executive, to name a few. The goal, according to the CEO, was to issue twelve to fifteen new cards a year.

American Express market share today: 18 percent.

Levi Strauss has done the same with blue jeans. In order to appeal to a wider market, Levi introduced a plethora of different styles and cuts, including baggy, zippered, and wide-leg jeans. At one point, Levi's jeans were available in twenty-seven different cuts. And if you could not find a pair of jeans off the rack to fit, Levi's would even custom cut jeans to your exact measurements. Yet over the past seven years the company's share of the denim jeans market has fallen from 31 to 19 percent.

Procter & Gamble has done the same with toothpaste.

When we worked for Crest, the marketing manager asked us, "Crest has thirty-eight SKUs. Do you think that's too many or too few?"

"How many teeth do you have in your mouth?" we asked.

"Thirty-two."

"No toothpaste should have more stock-keeping units than teeth in one's mouth," we responded.

When we were asked that question, Crest had 36 percent of the market. Today the brand has more than fifty SKUs, but its market share has declined to 25 percent. And not surprisingly, Crest has lost its leadership to Colgate.

Many companies try to justify line extension by invoking the masterbrand, superbrand, or megabrand concept.

- Chevrolet is the megabrand and Camaro, Caprice, Cavalier, Corsica-Beretta, Corvette, Lumina, Malibu, Metro, Monte Carlo, and Prizm are the individual brands.

- Pontiac is the megabrand and Bonneville, Firebird, Grand Am, Grand Prix, and Sunfire are the individual brands.

- Oldsmobile is the megabrand and Achieva, Aurora, Ciera, Cutlass Supreme, Intrigue, Eighty Eight, and Ninety Eight are the individual brands.

But people don't think this way. In their minds, most people try to assign one brand name to each product. And they are not consistent in how they assign such names. They tend to use the name that best captures the essence of the product. It could be the megabrand name. Or the model name. Or a nickname.

The Lumina owner will say, "I drive a Chevrolet." The Corvette owner will say, "I drive a Vette."

There are thousands of tiny teeter-totters in the consumer's mind. And like their real-life counterparts, both sides can't be up at the same time. On the Chevrolet/ Lumina teeter-totter, the Chevrolet side is up, so the car owner says, "I drive a Chevrolet." On the Chevrolet/ Corvette teeter-totter, the Corvette side is up, so the Corvette owner says, "I drive a Vette."

Marketers constantly run branding programs that are in conflict with how people want to perceive their brands. Customers want brands that are narrow in scope and are distinguishable by a single word, the shorter the better.

But marketers, in an effort to distinguish their products from other similar products in the marketplace, launch ridiculously overzealous brand names:

- Vaseline Intensive Care suntan lotion
- Neutrogena oil-free acne wash
- Gillette ClearGel antiperspirant
- Johnson's Clean & Clear oil-free foaming facial cleanser
- St. Joseph aspirin-free tablets for adults
- Kleenex Super Dry baby diapers
- Fruit of the Loom laundry detergent
- Harley-Davidson wine coolers
- Heinz all-natural cleaning vinegar

Marketers often confuse the power of a brand with the sales generated by that brand. But sales are not just a function of a brand's power. Sales are also a function of the strength or weakness of a brand's competition.

If your competition is weak or nonexistent, you can often increase sales by weakening your brand. That is, by expanding it over more segments of the market. You therefore can draw the conclusion that line extension works.

But in so doing, the only thing you have demonstrated is the weakness of the competition. Coca-Cola had nothing to lose when it launched Diet Coke, because the competition (Pepsi-Cola) also had a line-extended product called Diet Pepsi.

While extending the line might bring added sales in the short term, it runs counter to the notion of branding. If

you want to build a powerful brand in the minds of consumers, you need to contract your brand, not expand it. In
the long term, expanding your brand will diminish your
power and weaken your image.

**In a few short years, Starbucks has become
one of America's best known and most popular
brands. Narrowing one's focus is not the same
as carrying a limited line. Starbucks offers
thirty different types of coffee.**

2
The Law of Contraction

*A brand becomes stronger when
you narrow its focus.*

Every small town in America has a coffee shop. In larger cities and towns you can find coffee shops on every other block.

So what can you find to eat in a coffee shop? Everything. Breakfast, lunch, dinner. Pancakes, muffins, hot dogs, hamburgers, sandwiches, pie, ice cream, and, of course, coffee.

What did Howard Schultz do? In an incredible burst of business creativity, he opened a coffee shop that specialized in, of all things, coffee. In other words, he narrowed the focus.

Today Schultz's brainchild, Starbucks, is a rapidly growing chain that does hundreds of millions of dollars' worth of business annually. His company, Starbucks Corp., is worth more than a billion dollars on the stock market. And Schultz's share of that stock is worth $65 million.

Every small town in America has a delicatessen. In larger cities and towns, you can find delis in every neighborhood.

So what can you find to eat in a delicatessen? Everything. Soups, salads, hot and cold sandwiches, three types of roast beef, four types of ham, five types of cheese. Hard rolls, soft rolls, hero rolls, three types of pickles, four types of bread, five types of bagels. Potato chips, pretzels, corn chips. Muffins, doughnuts, cookies, cakes, candy bars, ice cream, frozen yogurt. Beer, soda, water, coffee, tea, soft drinks of all varieties. Newspapers, cigarettes, lottery tickets. Every decent delicatessen prides itself on carrying everything.

What did Fred DeLuca do? He narrowed the focus to one type of sandwich, the submarine sandwich.

Good things happen when you contract your brand rather than expand it. The first stroke of genius in DeLuca's case was in coming up with the name.

Fred DeLuca called his chain Subway, a great name for a store that sold just submarine sandwiches. It was a name that no consumer could forget.

The second smart move concerned operations. When you make only submarine sandwiches, you get pretty good at making submarine sandwiches.

The Law of Contraction

The average McDonald's has sixty or seventy individual items on the menu. Half the employees are teenagers, not yet old or mature enough to handle the complexities of today's operation. And people wonder why the food and service aren't as good as when it just served hamburgers, french fries, and soft drinks. (The original McDonald's menu had just eleven items, including all sizes and flavors.)

Subway has become the eighth-largest fast-food chain in the United States. The company has more than 13,000 units worldwide. Since Subway is a private company, we don't know exactly how profitable it is, but we do know how much money Fred DeLuca has been paying himself. (He was forced to disclose his salary in a court case.)

In 1990, Fred DeLuca paid himself $27 million. In 1991, $32 million. In 1992, $42 million. In 1993, $54 million. In 1994, $60 million. That's a lot of dough for making submarine sandwiches.

Charles Lazarus owned one store, called Children's Supermart, which sold two things: children's furniture and toys. But he wanted to grow.

What is the conventional way to grow? Adding more things to sell. Sure, he could have added bicycles, baby food, diapers, and children's clothing to the store. But he didn't.

Lazarus actually threw out the furniture and focused on the toys.

Good things happen when you contract your brand

rather than expand it. First he filled the empty half of the store with more toys, giving the buyer a greater selection and more reason to visit the store. Then, instead of calling it Children's Supermart, Lazarus called his place Toys "R" Us.

Today Toys "R" Us sells 20 percent of all the toys sold in the United States. And the chain has become the model for the specialty stores or category killers on the retail scene. Home Depot in home supplies. The Gap in everyday casual clothing. The Limited in clothes for working women. Victoria's Secret in ladies' lingerie. PetsMart in pet supplies. Blockbuster Video in video rentals. CompUSA in computers. Foot Locker in athletic shoes.

Good things happen when you contract rather than expand your business. Most retail category killers follow the same five-step pattern.

1. Narrow the focus. A powerful branding program always starts by contracting the category, not expanding it.

2. Stock in depth. A typical Toys "R" Us carries 10,000 toys versus 3,000 toys for even a large department store.

3. Buy cheap. Toys "R" Us makes its money buying toys, not selling toys.

4. Sell cheap. When you can buy cheap, you can sell cheap and still maintain good margins.

5. Dominate the category. The ultimate objective of any branding program is to dominate a category.

When you dominate a category, you become extremely powerful. Microsoft has 90 percent of the worldwide market for desktop computer operating systems. Intel has 80 percent of the worldwide market for microprocessors. Coca-Cola has 70 percent of the worldwide market for cola. And in order to dominate a category, you must narrow your brand's focus.

Why then do so few marketers want to contract their brands? Why do most marketers want to expand their brands? Because people look at successful companies and are led astray. They assume that companies are successful because they are expanding. (Starbucks, for example, currently is busy getting into everything from ice cream to bottled drinks to tea.)

But let's focus on you for a moment. Let's say that you really want to be rich. Now ask yourself: Can I get rich by doing what rich people do?

Rich people buy expensive houses and eat in expensive restaurants. They drive Rolls-Royces and wear Rolex watches. They vacation on the Riviera.

Would buying an expensive house, a Rolls-Royce, and a Rolex make you rich? Just the opposite. It's likely to make you poor, even bankrupt.

Most people search for success in all the wrong places. They try to find out what rich and successful companies are currently doing and then try to copy them.

What do rich companies do? They buy Gulfstream jets. They run programs like empowerment, leadership training, open-book management, and total-quality management. And they extend their brands.

Will buying a Gulfstream jet for $38 million make your company successful? Unlikely. Will extending your brand? Just as unlikely.

If you want to be rich, you have to do what rich people did before they were rich—you have to find out what they did to become rich. If you want to have a successful company, you have to do what successful companies did before they were successful.

As it happens, they all did the same thing. They narrowed their focus.

When Domino's Pizza first got started, it sold pizza and submarine sandwiches. When Little Caesars first got started, it sold pizza, fried shrimp, fish and chips, and roasted chicken. When Papa John's first got started, it sold pizza, cheesesteaks, submarine sandwiches, fried mushrooms, fried zucchini, salads, and onion rings.

Now how do you suppose Tom Monaghan, Michael and

Marian Ilitch and John Schnatter built Domino's Pizza,
Little Caesars, and Papa John's into big powerful brands?
By expanding their menus or contracting them?

Good things happen when you narrow the focus.

THE BODY SHOP

Anita Roddick created the Body Shop in 1976 around the concept of "natural" cosmetics, made of pure ingredients, not tested on animals, and kind to both the environment and the people indigenous to the communities in which the products originated. With virtually no advertising, but with massive amounts of publicity, the Body Shop has become a powerful global brand.

3

The Law of Publicity

*The birth of a brand is achieved
with publicity, not advertising.*

Most of America's 5,208 advertising agencies are com-
mitted to the concept of building a brand with advertising.

"The fundamental thing we're all about is building
brand leaders," said the chief executive of D'Arcy Masius
Benton & Bowles recently. "The way to do that is to have
a superior understanding of the consumer, which leads to
better, fresher, more powerful creative work that ultimately builds brands."

*Building brand leaders with better, fresher creative
work?* We think not. Most marketers confuse brand
building with brand maintenance. While a hefty advertising budget might be needed to maintain high-flying
brands like McDonald's and Coca-Cola, advertising generally won't get a new brand off the ground.

Anita Roddick built the Body Shop into a major brand with no advertising. Instead she traveled the world on a relentless quest for publicity, pushing her ideas about the environment. It was the endless torrent of newspaper and magazine articles, plus radio and television interviews, that literally created the Body Shop brand.

Starbucks doesn't spend a hill of beans on advertising either. In ten years, the company has spent less than $10 million on advertising, a trivial amount for a brand that delivers annual sales approaching a billion dollars.

Wal-Mart became the world's largest retailer with sales approaching $100 billion with very little advertising. A Wal-Mart sibling, Sam's Club, averages $45 million per store with almost no advertising.

On the other hand, Miller Brewing spent $50 million to launch a brand called Miller Regular. (Or just plain Miller.) The brand generated no publicity, almost no perceptions in the minds of beer drinkers, and very little sales—$50 million down the drain.

Would better, fresher creative work have built a beer called Miller Regular into a brand leader? We think not. There is no publicity potential in a regular beer with a line-extended name like Miller.

In the past, it may have been true that a beefy advertising budget was the key ingredient in the brand-building process. But what worked in the past doesn't necessarily work today. We live in an overcommunicated society, where each of us gets hit with hundreds of commercial messages daily.

Today brands are born, not made. A new brand must be capable of generating favorable publicity in the media or it won't have a chance in the marketplace.

And just how do you generate publicity? The best way to generate publicity is by being first. In other words, by being the first brand in a new category.

- Band-Aid, the first adhesive bandage.
- Charles Schwab, the first discount stockbrokerage firm.
- CNN, the first cable news network.
- Compaq, the first portable personal computer.
- Domino's, the first home delivery pizza chain.
- ESPN, the first cable sports network.
- Gore-Tex, the first breathable waterproof cloth.
- Heineken, the first imported beer.
- Hertz, the first car-rental company.
- Intel, the first microprocessor.
- Jell-O, the first gelatin dessert.
- Kentucky Fried Chicken, the first fast-food chicken chain.
- *National Enquirer*, the first supermarket tabloid.
- *Playboy*, the first men's magazine.
- Q-Tips, the first cotton swab.
- Reynolds Wrap, the first aluminum foil.

- Rollerblade, the first in-line skate.
- Samuel Adams, the first microbrewed beer.
- Saran Wrap, the first plastic food wrap.
- Sun Microsystems, the first Unix workstation.
- Tide, the first detergent.
- *Time,* the first weekly news magazine.
- Xerox, the first plain-paper copier.

All of these brands (and many, many more) were first in a new category and, in the process, generated enormous amounts of publicity.

There's a strong relationship between the two. The news media wants to talk about what's new, what's first, and what's hot, not what's better. When your brand can make news, it has a chance to generate publicity. And the best way to make news is to announce a new category, not a new product.

What others say about your brand is so much more powerful than what you can say about it yourself. That's why publicity in general is more powerful than advertising. And why over the past two decades, public relations has eclipsed advertising as the most powerful force in branding.

Yet for years public relations has been treated as a secondary function to advertising. PR people even used to measure their successes in terms of advertising space. Publicity stories were converted into equivalent advertising expenditures.

Even worse, marketing strategies were usually formulated first into advertising slogans. Then the public relations people were asked to reinforce the advertising by creating PR programs to communicate the slogans.

Not anymore. Today brands are built with publicity and maintained with advertising. The cart is now driving the horse.

So why hasn't the ascendancy of PR made news in the media? Why are public relations departments in most companies still subservient to advertising departments? Why are eight of the top ten public relations firms still owned by advertising agencies instead of vice versa?

Why has the media ignored the biggest story in marketing?

It's the grass phenomenon. Nobody ever notices the grass growing or pays attention to a trend that is slow in developing.

Take the facsimile, for example. Over the past two decades, the facsimile has become an indispensable part of every company's communication portfolio. Americans will send 65 billion pages of faxes this year, more than 240 per person. And 50 percent of all international phone calls are now fax calls.

Yet we don't remember a single article in any of the major management publications on the rise of the facsimile. It happened too slowly.

On the other hand, the opposite is true of the Internet. The rise of the Internet happened so quickly that it created a blaze of publicity. And yet, even today, the average executive is more likely to send a fax than an e-mail.

Advertising executives in particular are inclined to slight public relations. "If the advertising is brilliant, the PR will fall out of that," said one particularly brilliant advertising executive recently.

But what works in branding today is publicity, not advertising. This is especially true in the high-tech field. All of the big global marketing powerhouses—Microsoft, Intel, Dell, Compaq, Gateway, Oracle, Cisco, SAP, and Sun Microsystems—were first created in the pages of *The Wall Street Journal, Business Week, Forbes,* and *Fortune.* By publicity, not by advertising.

Years ago we worked with Lotus Development Corp. on branding strategy for Lotus Notes. The essence of the strategy was the promotion of Notes as "the first successful *groupware* product." With, of course, the emphasis on "groupware."

This idea caught on like crazy with the media, which ran story after story on the new groupware concept. Yet typically the Lotus advertising people ignored the group-ware idea in favor of nonsensical advertising pabulum.

It didn't matter because public relations is more important than advertising. As a result of the publicity program, Notes became an enormous success and as a result IBM paid the astounding price of $3.5 billion for Lotus Development Corp.

Most companies develop their branding strategies as if advertising were their primary communications vehicle. They're wrong. Strategy should be developed first from a publicity point of view.

**A consistent theme of Goodyear
advertising over the years has been
"#1 in tires." So who makes the
best tires? "It must be Goodyear," thinks
the consumer. "It's the leader."**

4
The Law of Advertising

Once born, a brand needs advertising
to stay healthy.

Your advertising budget is like a country's defense budget. Those massive advertising dollars don't buy you anything; they just keep you from losing market share to your competition.

All of those tanks, planes, and missiles just keep a country from being overrun by one of its enemies.

Publicity is a powerful tool, but sooner or later a brand outlives its publicity potential. The process normally goes through two distinct phases.

Phase one involves the introduction of the new category—the plain-paper copier, for example, introduced by Xerox in 1959. Hundreds of magazine and newspaper articles were written about the launch of the 914 copier. Xerox executives also appeared on numerous television shows to demonstrate their new baby. Much was written on the potential of the new category.

Phase two concerns the rise of the company that pioneered the new category. Again, hundred of articles were written about the marketing and financial successes of Xerox, a company that rose from the ashes of Haloid, a manufacturer of photographic paper.

Today, everybody knows that Xerox pioneered xerography and has become a global leader in copiers. There's no news story left to tell, so advertising takes over.

Almost every successful brand goes through the same process. Brands like Compaq, Dell, SAP, Oracle, Cisco, Microsoft, Starbucks, and Wal-Mart were born in a blaze of publicity. As the publicity dies out, each of these brands will someday have to shift to massive advertising to defend its position. First publicity, then advertising is the general rule.

Anybody who thinks advertising built Microsoft into a macrobrand should go back and read Chapter 3 again.

Sooner or later a leader has to shift its branding strategy from publicity to advertising. By raising the price of admission, advertising makes it difficult for a competitor to carve out a substantial share of the market.

To attack a heavily defended neighboring country requires substantial military expenditures. To attack a heavily defended brand leader like Coca-Cola, Nike, or McDonald's requires substantial marketing expenditures.

Leaders should not look on their advertising budgets as

investments that will pay dividends. Instead leaders should look on their advertising budgets as insurance that will protect them against losses caused by competitive attacks.

What should a brand leader advertise? Brand leadership, of course. Leadership is the single most important motivating factor in customer behavior.

- Heinz, America's favorite ketchup.
- Heineken, America's leading imported beer.
- Coca-Cola, the real thing.
- Visa, the #1 credit card in the world.
- Barilla, Italy's #1 pasta.
- Goodyear, #1 in tires.

The list of leaders that advertise their leadership is very short. Most leaders advertise some aspect of their quality.

But what happens when your advertising says, "Our product is better"? What does the reader, the viewer, or the listener to the advertisement really think when you make the claim that you produce a better product?

"That's what they all say."

Pick up a copy of any magazine or newspaper and flip through the advertisements. Almost every ad makes some type of better product claim. That's what they all say.

But what happens when your advertising says, "Our product is the leader"? What does the prospect think?

"It must be better."

Who makes the best ketchup in America? Do you really believe Hunt's is the best? You might, but most people believe that Heinz is the best. Why?

Heinz is the leader and everybody knows that in this freedom-loving, democratic, equal-opportunity country of ours, the better product always wins.

"I pledge allegiance to the flag of the United States of America, the republic for which it stands, and the leading brand in each category."

As yet, we Americans don't do the pledge of brand allegiance, but we might as well. That's how strong our belief is in the notion that the better brand will win.

Then why, you may ask, don't more advertisers advertise leadership? (Such claims are quite rare.)

They do consumer research. They ask customers why they buy the brands they buy. And people are quick to reply that they would never buy a brand just because it's the leader. As a matter of fact, they go out of their way to deny it.

"I never buy a brand just because it's the leader."

Then why did you choose the leading brand? Why do you drink Coca-Cola? Or rent from Hertz? Or attend Harvard University?

"Because it's better."

And now we have completed the circle. Everyone knows the better product will win in the marketplace. Since most people want to buy the better product, most people buy the leading brand. Which in turn keeps that brand the leader and gives the brand the perception that it's the better product.

Advertising is a powerful tool, not to build leadership of a fledgling brand, but to maintain that leadership once it is obtained. Companies that want to protect their well-established brands should not hesitate to use massive advertising programs to smother the competition.

Indeed, advertising is expensive. Today it takes $1.2 million to buy thirty seconds during the Super Bowl. And top-rated prime-time shows are equally ridiculous from a monetary point of view.

So why spend the money?

Advertising may not pay for itself, but if you're the leader, advertising will make your competitor pay through the nose for the privilege of competing with you. Many won't be able to afford it; those who can won't bother. Instead they'll be content to nibble on the crumbs around your huge piece of the pie.

**Federal Express became successful by
being the first air cargo carrier to narrow its
focus to overnight delivery, thereby owning the
word "overnight" in the mind of the air cargo
user. FedEx has become synonymous with
overnight delivery.**

5

The Law of the Word

*A brand should strive to own a word
in the mind of the consumer.*

What comes to mind when you think about owning a
Mercedes?

If you could pry open the mind of the typical automobile
buyer, you would probably find the word "prestige" closely
identified with the brand. Tell the truth, don't you associate
prestige with the Mercedes-Benz brand? Most people do.

You might also associate attributes like *expensive, German, well engineered,* and *reliable* with the brand, but the
core differentiation is prestige. Lamborghinis are expensive, Audis are German, Hondas are well engineered, and
Toyotas are reliable, but none of these brands conveys the
prestige of a Mercedes.

If you want to build a brand, you must focus your
branding efforts on owning a word in the prospect's mind.
A word that nobody else owns.

What prestige is to Mercedes, safety is to Volvo.

Volvo owns the word "safety" in the mind of the automobile buyer. And, as a result, over the past decade Volvo has become the largest-selling European luxury car in America.

Once a brand owns a word, it's almost impossible for a competitor to take that word away from the brand. Could you build a safer car than a Volvo? Probably. Many brands have already claimed to do so, including Saab and Mercedes-Benz. Could another brand own the word "safety" in the mind? Probably not.

What comes to mind when you think about owning a BMW?

A car that's fun to drive. The ultimate driving machine. BMW owns the word "driving" in the mind. And, as a result, BMW has become the second-largest-selling European luxury car in America.

Yet none of these three brands (Mercedes, Volvo, and BMW) is a perfect example of the law of the word since they have all recently violated the law of expansion. Mercedes has moved into less expensive, less prestigious cars. Volvo into sporty cars. And BMW into more luxurious cars.

And so it goes. The minute a brand begins to stand for something in the mind, the company usually looks for ways to broaden the base, to get into other markets, to capture other attributes. This is a serious error and one of the most common mistakes in branding.

The Law of the Word

What's a Kleenex? What word do you associate with the Kleenex brand?

On the surface, Kleenex seems unfocused. It's soft and pops up; it's well known and comes in many different forms. There are sport Kleenexes, family-size Kleenexes, psychedelic Kleenexes. Yet Kleenex is by far the leading brand of pocket tissue.

What word does Kleenex own in the mind? Kleenex owns the category word. *Kleenex is tissue*.

Kleenex was the first pocket tissue. Before Kimberly-Clark introduced Kleenex, there was no market for a pocket tissue. But instead of expanding to toilet tissue and paper towels, Kleenex kept hammering away at its original focus.

"Don't put a cold in your pocket," was the marketing message for many years. The pocket handkerchief virtually disappeared from the market, replaced by Kleenex tissues in their many variations.

Why don't the many varieties of tissue dilute the Kleenex brand? Because when a person looks across a room, sees a box of Scott tissue, and says: "Please hand me a Kleenex," you know you have a solid brand locked into the mind of the consumer.

In the same way that Kleenex owns tissue, Jell-O owns gelatin dessert, Coca-Cola owns cola, Band-Aid owns adhesive bandage, Saran Wrap owns plastic food film and Rollerblade owns in-line skates.

You know your brand owns the category name when people use your brand name generically.

"Make me a Xerox copy."

"I need a Q-Tip."

"Cover the plate with Reynolds Wrap."

"Hand me the Scotch tape."

Nor is it any secret how these brands managed to own the category word. They were first, plain and simple.

Here's the catch: You can't become generic by overtaking the leader. Pepsi won't become generic for cola even if the brand outsells Coke (as it once did in the supermarket distribution channel). You can only become generic by being the first brand and establishing the category.

So what do you do if you weren't the first in a category? Quite often you can create a new category by simply narrowing your focus.

Emery Air Freight, started in 1946, was the first air cargo carrier. But Emery fell into the Chevrolet trap. Instead of focusing on one type of service, it offered everything. Overnight, inexpensive two- or three-day service, small packages, large packages. "Whatever you want to ship, Emery can handle it."

What did Federal Express do? In the early seventies, it was a struggling player in the delivery business. But in a streak of brilliance, CEO Fred Smith decided to narrow the focus to overnight delivery only. "When it absolutely, positively has to be there overnight."

Today Federal Express is a much larger company than Emery (now called Emery Worldwide). And "FedEx" has become the generic term for overnight delivery.

"FedEx this package to the Coast."

What word does Federal Express own in the mind? "Overnight," of course.

So what did Federal Express do next? It went global, where the very thing it had become known for, overnight delivery, is impossible. (Five o'clock in the afternoon in New York is already tomorrow morning in Singapore.) And it got into less expensive two- and three-day delivery. And recently it bought a trucking company.

Virtually every marketing move Federal Express has made in the last dozen years has moved the company further away from the overnight concept.

Does this expansion hurt the brand? Yes. Does it hurt the company? Maybe not, as long as there are no competitors astute enough to narrow the focus and put the same squeeze on Federal Express that Federal Express put on Emery Air Freight.

Look what Prego did to Ragú. For years Ragú was the leading brand of spaghetti sauce with a market share in excess of 50 percent. Like Emery Air Freight, Ragú had many different varieties.

So what did Prego do? The brand narrowed its focus to one variety, "thick" spaghetti sauce. With this one type of sauce Prego won 27 percent of the market. Prego owns the word "thick" in the mind of the spaghetti sauce buyer.

The same principle holds true in many different categories, no matter how narrow or obscure the industry. In the financial world, a "Bloomberg" is a terminal that provides analytical tools as well as instant business news and stock prices. Bloomberg LP was the first company to introduce a device that would help money managers contrast and compare financial data.

Words are the key to brand building. Reality, of course, rests in a visual world of shapes, colors, textures, and dimensions. But reality has no meaning without the context provided by the human mind. The mind gives meaning to visual reality by using words. Only when the mind thinks that an object is large or small, beautiful or ugly, dark or light, does that meaning arise.

The same is true of the product or service you are selling. The product itself might have a visual reality. But it's the brand name and its associations that give the product meaning in the consumer's mind.

So you can forget about the laundry list of wonderful attributes your product has. You can't possibly associate them all with your brand name in a human mind. To get into the consumer's mind you have to sacrifice. You have to reduce the essence of your brand to a single thought or attribute. An attribute that nobody else already owns in your category.

The average adult knows the meanings of perhaps 50,000 words. Yet there are more than a million registered trademarks. And you want your trademark to stand for how many different attributes in the mind?

Until science figures out a way to replace human brain tissue with silicon chips, it's a physical impossibility for most brands to go beyond a single word. Consider your-self lucky if your brand can own a word like "safety" or "driving" or "thick" or "overnight."

Many marketers know this and they still look to expand the meanings of their brands. Why?

Growth. They feel trapped in their present positions. They want to grow, so they feel they have no choice but to expand their brands.

But what works is not expanding the brand, but expand-ing the market. In other words, instead of moving from overnight to two- or three-day delivery, Federal Express expanded the market for overnight delivery.

By focusing on overnight, Federal Express was able to make overnight the in-thing among business executives. As a result of its high price and flashy packaging, people thought, "Hey, this package must be important because it came via Federal Express."

And overnight deliveries boomed along with the for-tunes of Federal Express.

Mercedes employed a similar strategy. What was the market for expensive automobiles before Mercedes-Benz? Teeny-tiny.

Mercedes built the market for expensive cars by using prestige as its strategy. But you need subtlety in dealing with a word like "prestige." Its connotations may work in brand building, but the word itself does not. It's not that people aren't dying to own prestige brands. They just hate to admit it.

To be successful in branding a "prestige" product or service, you need to do two things:

1. You need to make your product or service more expensive than the competition.

2. You need to find a code word for prestige.

The first part was easy. Mercedes-Benz priced its vehicles at about twice the price of a comparable Cadillac. ("Mercedes cars must be better than Cadillacs," thinks the buyer, "because they are twice as expensive.")

Mercedes also found a powerful code word for prestige. "Engineered like no other car in the world."

What overnight did for Federal Express, engineering did for Mercedes. It expanded the market by giving the owner an excuse to buy an expensive, prestigious car. Instead of a Cadillac, the car of choice for the country club crowd became a Mercedes.

But also like Federal Express, Mercedes has started expanding the brand with cheap sports cars, inexpensive sedans, and sport utility vehicles. With a name like Mercedes-Benz, a reputation like Mercedes-Benz, and a history like Mercedes-Benz (the company invented the automobile), the brand should be the largest-selling luxury car in America. But it's not.

Go back in history. By far the most successful brands are those that kept a narrow focus and then expanded the category as opposed to those brands that tried to expand their names into other categories.

What was the market for expensive pens before Montblanc? Minuscule.

What was the market for expensive vodka before Stolichnaya and Absolut? Nil.

What was the market for safe cars before Volvo? Zip.

If "what is the size of the market?" is the first question your company asks itself, then it is taking the wrong road to success.

Ask not what percentage of an existing market your brand can achieve, ask how large a market your brand can create by narrowing its focus and owning a word in the mind.

Coca-Cola

In 1942, Coca-Cola launched an advertising program called "The only thing like Coca-Cola is Coca-Cola itself. It's the real thing." In 1970, it reprised the "real thing" slogan for about a year.

6
The Law of Credentials

The crucial ingredient in the success of any brand is its claim to authenticity.

Customers are suspicious. They tend to disbelieve most product claims. Your brand might last longer, require less maintenance, and be easier to use, but who will accept claims like these?

There is one claim, however, that should take precedence over every other claim. It's the one claim that elevates the brand above the competition. And makes every other claim much more believable.

It's the real thing. It's the claim to authenticity.

When Coca-Cola first made this claim customers instantly responded. "Yes," they agreed. "Coke is the real thing. Everything else is an imitation."

Even though the last "real thing" advertising ran almost thirty years ago, the concept has become closely associated with Coca-Cola. It's the brand's credentials.

Even today, "the real thing" is so closely associated with Coca-Cola that newspaper and magazine reporters will try to work these words into almost every article written about the company.

Credentials are the collateral you put up to guarantee the performance of your brand. When you have the right credentials, your prospect is likely to believe almost anything you say about your brand.

Leadership is the most direct way to establish the credentials of a brand. Coca-Cola, Hertz, Heinz, Visa, and Kodak all have credentials because they are widely perceived to be the leading brands in their categories. When you don't have the leading brand, your best strategy is to create a new category in which you can claim leadership.

Which is what Polaroid did when it became the leader in the new category of instant photography. Yet when it tried to tackle Kodak in conventional photographic film, Polaroid failed miserably.

Many marketers attribute Polaroid's failure to the fact that the brand couldn't be "stretched" from instant to conventional 35mm film. While true, this conclusion doesn't really describe the dynamics involved.

The simple fact is that Polaroid has no credentials in conventional 35mm film. Why buy your conventional film from Polaroid when Kodak is the expert in this category? Only if you want instant film will you buy Polaroid; it knows instant photography.

The Law of Credentials

A number of years ago, Patrick Sullivan (currently CEO of SalesLogix) arrived in our offices with a software product called Act. "What does Act do?" we asked.

"Everything," Pat replied. "Act keeps track of your calendar, your correspondence, your mailing lists and your expense accounts. Act literally does everything."

Not a good direction. We wanted to find the one thing we could use to build a new category. After much discussion the group decided that the new software could best be described as "contact" software. In other words, software designed for salespeople and others who do contact work.

"The largest-selling contact software" became the credentials for the new brand. Everywhere the brand name was used, the credentials were also used. In advertising, publicity, brochures, letterheads, calling cards. Even on the product box itself.

Today, Act has 70 percent of the contact software market and has become the dominant brand in the category.

Credentials are particularly important in the publicity process. Reporters and editors are quick to dismiss advertising claims as puffery. But they readily acknowledge leadership and other aspects related to a brand's credentials.

- If a reporter is doing a car-rental story, who is he or she likely to call first? Hertz, exactly.

- If a reporter is doing a cola story, he or she will almost always call Coca-Cola.
- If a reporter is doing a computer software story, he or she will probably call Microsoft.

Many companies run branding programs almost devoid of credentials. If you leaf through a stack of print ads or watch a series of television commercials, you'll find an endless parade of almost meaningless benefits: Tastes great, saves money, whitens teeth, easy assembly, bigger, smaller, lighter, faster, cheaper. While many of the benefits may be of intense interest to prospective customers, they each lack credibility so they are generally ignored. "That's what they all say."

When the benefits, however, are structured around some aspect of a brand's credentials, they carry much more weight.

If Act claims to make you more productive on the road and cut your paperwork in half, then you tend to believe these claims because "Act is the largest-selling contact software."

Datastream did the same thing in maintenance software. Early on, Datastream found itself with 50 percent of the market. Granted the market was small. Very, very small.

No matter. Datastream promoted itself as "the leader in maintenance software." This same leadership theme was used in all of Datastream's literature. Today, the market has exploded and Datastream still dominates the category. It truly is the leader in maintenance software.

Conventional thinking would have it otherwise. "The market is small. Nobody cares that we're the leader. They don't even care about maintenance software itself, otherwise they would be buying more of these kinds of products. Forget leadership. We have to concentrate all of our efforts on selling the benefits of the category."

Never forget leadership. No matter how small the market, don't get duped into simply selling the benefits of the category.

There are also the long-term benefits of leadership. Because once you get on top, it's hard to lose your spot. A widely publicized study of twenty-five leading brands in twenty-five different product categories in the year 1923 showed that twenty of the same twenty-five brands are still the leaders in their categories today. In seventy-five years only five brands lost their leadership.

Never assume that people know which brand is the leader. This is especially true in fast-growing, new categories like contact software and maintenance software. Most new prospects have no experience with the category and little knowledge of available brands, so they naturally gravitate to the leading brand.

As the category matures, customers become more adventuresome and more willing to try different brands that offer seemingly unique advantages. Leaders often have to write off the more sophisticated customers who will go out of their way not to buy the leading brand.

Write them off. You can't appeal to everybody.

Not all brands can be leaders, although every category offers a wealth of possibilities. Take beer, for example. Here are some categories for leadership credentials:

- The leading beer.
- The leading light beer.
- The leading imported beer.
- The leading microbrew.
- The leading ice beer.
- The leading high-priced beer.
- The leading Mexican beer.
- The leading German beer.
- The leading Canadian beer.
- The leading Japanese beer.

For almost all of the hundreds of companies we have worked with around the world, we have found some credentials that could be exploited. If not, we created the credentials by inventing a new category.

You see credentials at work in everyday life. How many times have you walked away from a new restaurant because it was almost empty? Most people prefer to wait

The Law of Credentials

for a table at a restaurant that is crowded, rather than eat in an empty one. If this place was really good (goes the thinking), there would be a line out the door.

That's the power of credentials.

♔
ROLEX

Rolex has become the world's best-known and best-selling brand of expensive watch. Does quality have anything to do with its success? Probably not. Does Rolex make high-quality watches? Probably. Does it matter? Probably not.

7

The Law of Quality

Quality is important, but brands are not built by quality alone.

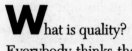hat is quality?

Everybody thinks they can tell a high-quality product from a low-quality one, but in reality things are not always so obvious.

- Does a Rolex keep better time than a Timex? Are you sure?

- Does a Leica take better pictures than a Pentax? Are you sure?

- Does a Mercedes have fewer mechanical problems than a Cadillac? Are you sure?

- Does Hertz have better service than Alamo? Are you sure?

- Does a Montblanc pen write better than a Cross? Are you sure?

- Does Coca-Cola taste better than Pepsi-Cola? Most people seem to think so because Coke outsells Pepsi. Yet in taste tests in the US most people prefer the taste of Pepsi.

Common wisdom blames the testing procedures. If Coke outsells Pepsi, there must be something wrong with a taste test that shows the opposite.

Quality is a concept that has thousands of adherents. The way to build a better brand, goes the thinking, is by building a better-quality product.

What seems so intuitively true in theory is not always so in practice. Building your brand on quality is like building your house on sand. You can build quality into your product, but that has little to do with your success in the marketplace.

Years of observation have led us to this conclusion. There is almost no correlation between success in the marketplace and success in comparative testing of brands—whether it be taste tests, accuracy tests, reliability tests, durability tests, or any other independent, objective third-party testing of brands.

Read *Consumer Reports*. And then check the sales rankings of the brands tested compared to the magazine's quality rankings. You will find little correlation. As a matter of fact, the magazine's success could be attributed to its ability to find little-known brands that outperform leading brands.

In a recent ranking of sixteen brands of small cars, the number-one brand in quality was twelfth in sales. The number-two brand in quality was ninth in sales. The number-three brand in quality was dead last in sales. If quality translates into sales, the numbers don't seem to show it.

Let's say you went shopping for an automobile tomorrow. Does quality matter? Absolutely. Most car buyers look for the best-quality car they can afford.

But where does the concept of quality reside? In the showroom? No.

Quality, or rather the perception of quality, resides in the mind of the buyer. If you want to build a powerful brand, you have to build a powerful perception of quality in the mind.

As it happens, the best way to build a quality perception in the mind is by following the laws of branding.

Take the law of contraction. What happens when you narrow your focus? You become a specialist rather than a generalist. And a specialist is generally perceived to know more, in other words to have "higher quality," than a generalist.

Does a cardiologist know more about the heart than a general practitioner of medicine? Most people think so. Certainly the perception is true. From a marketing point of view, it really doesn't matter.

Yet most companies want to be general practitioners. Why? They want to expand the market for their products and services. And in doing so they violate the law of expansion.

Another important aspect of brand building is having a better name. All other factors being equal, the brand with the better name will come out on top.

Being a specialist and having a better name go hand in hand. Expanding a brand and being a generalist tend to destroy your ability to select a powerful name.

There is much misinformation on this subject in business publications today. Omnibus brands are weak, not strong. General Electric, General Motors, and General Dynamics might be well known, but as brands they are weak because they're too broad in scope.

We know what you are thinking. Some of these omnibus brands are among the world's leading companies in terms of sales, profits, and stock market equity. And you're right. But a weak brand can in fact be a sales success if it competes with even weaker brands. Take General Electric. Most of GE's competitors are also omnibus brands like Westinghouse, General Motors, and United Technologies. Who wins when two weak brands compete? A weak brand that just happens to be less weak than its competitor.

When General Electric tried to compete in mainframe computers with a strong brand like IBM, the GE brand was a multimillion-dollar loser. About $300 million to be exact.

When General Electric tried to compete in household products, the GE brand was no match for the specialists.

(The products were subsequently sold to Black & Decker, which promptly proved that an omnibus brand like Black & Decker was no better than the GE brand.)

Mile-wide brands like General Electric and General Motors look strong, but in reality are weak. They look strong because they are well known and have been in business for decades. But when they go against the specialists, they are weak.

Another factor in building a high-quality perception is having a high price. Rolex, Häagen-Dazs, Mercedes-Benz, Rolls-Royce, Montblanc, Dom Pérignon, Chivas Regal, Absolut, Jack Daniel's, and Ritz-Carlton are all brands that benefit from their high price.

High price is a benefit to customers. It allows the affluent customer to obtain psychic satisfaction from the public purchase and consumption of a high-end brand.

The customer who wears a Rolex watch doesn't do so to be more punctual. The customer who wears a Rolex watch does so to let other people know that he or she can afford to buy a Rolex watch.

Why do blue jeans buyers pay $100 or more for a pair of Replay, Big Star, or Diesel jeans? And would they pay the price if the label were on the inside of the jeans instead of on the outside?

And what does the sommelier say to the restaurant customer who has just ordered an eighty-dollar bottle of wine? "We have a twenty-dollar bottle that tastes just as good"?

Not likely. Even if the restaurant did have a twenty-dollar bottle that tasted just as good. And even if the customer believed the twenty-dollar bottle tasted just as good.

Conventional wisdom often advocates marketing a high-quality product at a comparable price. This is usually what is meant by a quality strategy. This is what Ford means when it says, "Quality is Job 1." Everything else, including price, is equal, but we are going to win by having the better-quality automobile.

Not likely. Quality is a nice thing to have, but brands are not built by quality alone.

A better strategy in a sea of similar products with similar prices is to deliberately start with a higher price. Then ask yourself, What can we put into our brand to justify the higher price?

- Rolex made its watches bigger and heavier with a unique-looking wristband.
- Callaway made its drivers oversized.
- Montblanc made its pens fatter.
- Häagen-Dazs added more butterfat.
- Chivas Regal let its Scotch whiskey age longer.

There's nothing wrong with quality. We always advise our clients to build as much quality into their brands as they can afford. (Hey, it might save you money on service costs later on.) But don't count on quality alone to build your brand.

To build a quality brand you need to narrow the focus and combine that narrow focus with a better name and a higher price.

EatZi's is the first brand in a new category which it calls "the meal-market." Jointly owned by Brinker International and Phil Romano, EatZi's focuses on restaurant-quality food primarily for takeout consumption.

8
The Law of the Category

A leading brand should promote the category, not the brand.

According to the law of contraction a brand becomes stronger when you narrow its focus. What happens when you narrow the focus to such a degree that there is no longer any market for the brand?

This is potentially the best situation of all. What you have created is the opportunity to introduce a brand-new category.

- What was the market for an expensive vodka before Stolichnaya? Almost nothing.
- What was the market for expensive cars before Mercedes-Benz? Almost nothing.
- What was the market for cheap cars before Volkswagen? Almost nothing.

- What was the market for home pizza delivery before Domino's Pizza? Almost nothing.
- What was the market for in-line skates before Rollerblade? Almost nothing.

There's a paradox here. Branding is widely perceived as the process of capturing a bigger share of an existing market. Which is what is usually meant when the newly appointed CEO says, "We have to grow the business."

Yet the most efficient, most productive, most useful aspect of branding has nothing to do with increasing a company's market share.

The most efficient, most productive, most useful aspect of branding is creating a new category. In other words, narrowing the focus to nothing and starting something totally new.

That's the way to become the first brand in a new category and ultimately the leading brand in a rapidly growing new segment of the market.

To build a brand in a nonexisting category, to build something out of nothing, you have to do two things at once:

- You have to launch the brand in such a way as to create the perception that that brand was the first, the leader, the pioneer, or the original. Invariably, you should use one of these words to describe your brand.
- You have to promote the new category.

Isn't it easier to just promote the brand and forget about the category, you might be thinking. Easier, yes, but not as effective.

When Apple introduced its ill-fated Newton, it forgot about the category name. At first it called the Newton a "PDA," for personal digital assistant.

A notebook computer, a digital cell phone, or a digital watch can all be considered personal digital assistants. PDA did not distinguish the Newton from all those other personal digital assistants on the market.

You knew the Newton was in trouble when Apple ran big advertisements with the headline, "What is it?"

Better to answer that question *before* you launch a new brand rather than *after.*

Customers don't really care about new brands, they care about new categories. They don't care about Domino's; they care about whether or not their pizza will arrive in thirty minutes. They don't care about Callaway; they care about whether or not an oversize driver will cut strokes off their golf scores. They don't care about Prince; they care about whether or not an oversize racquet will improve their tennis game.

By first preempting the category (as Prince did with the oversize tennis racquet, Callaway did with the oversize driver, and Domino's did with home delivery of pizza) and then aggressively promoting the category, you create both a powerful brand and a rapidly escalating market. Callaway Golf outsells the next three brands combined.

EatZi's is trying to do the same thing in the restaurant business. Average annual sales of the units in operation are an astounding $14 million. (The highest-grossing restaurant in the world is reportedly Tavern on the Green in New York City's Central Park, which does in the neighborhood of $20 million a year.)

With only a handful of units in operation, EatZi's has created an incredible amount of excitement in the restaurant industry. Yet the concept is simplicity itself.

Last year, Americans spent $207 billion on restaurant meals, a sizable market. Of that total, 51 percent was spent for takeout or home delivery.

What Little Caesars did in pizza, EatZi's is doing in high-end white-tablecloth restaurant meals. Narrowing the focus to takeout only.

That's the way you build a brand. Narrow the focus to a slice of the market, whether it's pizza takeout or gourmet takeout. Then make your brand name stand for the category (the generic effect) at the same time that you expand the category by promoting the benefits of the category, not the brand.

What are the benefits of takeout pizza? It's the cheapest way to sell a pizza. No waiters or waitresses. No delivery trucks. As a result Little Caesars can sell a pizza cheaper than its competition. It captures this concept with its slogan, "Pizza. Pizza." Or the promise of two pizzas for the price of one.

EatZi's has yet to conceptualize the benefits of takeout beef Wellington, but that's what it should be working on. Promote the category, not the brand. What EatZi's calls the "meal-market" category.

When you're first, you can preempt the category. You are the only brand associated with the concept. You have a powerful publicity platform. You need to put your branding dollars behind the concept itself, so the concept will take off, pulling the brand along with it.

What happens when competition appears, as it inevitably does? Most category leaders just can't wait to shift into a brand-building mode. That's a mistake. Leaders should continue to promote the category, to increase the size of the pie rather than their slice of the pie.

Boston Chicken was a huge hit when it opened its doors. It was the first fast-food restaurant to focus on rotisserie chicken for the take-home dinner market. But instead of continuing to promote rotisserie chicken, it changed its name to Boston Market, added turkey, meat-loaf, and ham to the menu, and fell into trouble.

Leaders get antsy as their 100 percent share of the initial market drops to 90 and then to 80 or 70 percent as the market grows. "We've got to fight back and recapture our rightful share," they say.

The rightful share of a leading brand is never more than 50 percent. There's always room for a second brand and a passel of lesser brands. Instead of fighting competitive brands, a leader should fight competitive categories.

"Take the bus," category leader Greyhound once said, "and leave the driving to us."

"Take home your meals from EatZi's," the meal-market category leader could say, "and leave the cooking to us."

Contrary to popular belief, what would help EatZi's (and every category pioneer) is competition. Even though the leader's market share might decline, the rise of competitive brands can stimulate consumer interest in the category. (See Chapter 11, "The Law of Fellowship.")

One of Polaroid's biggest mistakes was forcing Kodak out of the instant-photography market. Although it won a few million in its lawsuit, Polaroid effectively removed a competitor that could have greatly expanded the market. (A Coke/Pepsi advertising war benefits both brands. It attracts media attention, which expands the consumer's interest in the cola category.)

Years ago, Johnson & Johnson, the leading brand of baby shampoo, mounted a major marketing campaign to sell the merits of its shampoo to adults. "You wash your hair every day, you need a mild shampoo. And what shampoo could be milder than a baby shampoo?"

Brilliant. At one point Johnson & Johnson baby shampoo became the number-one brand of adult shampoo. If other baby shampoo brands had jumped on the adult bandwagon, sales might have gone even higher.

Unfortunately for Johnson & Johnson, there *were* no other major baby shampoo brands.

Leading brands should promote the category, not the brand.

XEROX

One of the world's most powerful brands, Xerox demonstrates many of the most important laws of branding, including being the first in a new category (plain-paper copier) with a short, unique name. Yet when Xerox tried to put its powerful copier name on computers, the result was billions of dollars in losses.

9

The Law of the Name

*In the long run a brand is nothing
more than a name.*

The most important branding decision you will ever make is what to name your product or service. Because in the long run a brand is nothing more than a name.

Don't confuse what makes a brand successful in the short term with what makes a brand successful in the long term.

In the short term, a brand needs a unique idea or concept to survive. It needs to be first in a new category. It needs to own a word in the mind.

But in the long term, the unique idea or concept disappears. All that is left is the difference between your brand name and the brand names of your competitors.

Xerox was the first plain-paper copier. This unique idea built the powerful Xerox brand in the mind. But today all copiers are plain-paper copiers. The difference between brands is not in the products, but in the product names. Or rather the perception of the names.

In the beginning it was easy to sell a Xerox 914 copier.

All you had to do was show the difference between a Xerox copy and an ordinary copy. The Xerox copy was cleaner, sharper, and easier to read. The paper lay flat, felt better, and was much easier to handle and sort.

Today those differences are gone, but Xerox is still the best brand by far in the copier field. One reason is the name itself.

It's short, unique, and connotes high technology. The most valuable asset of the $19.5 billion Xerox Corporation is the Xerox name itself.

Yet marketers often disparage the importance of the name. "What really counts is the product itself and the benefits the product provides to our customers and prospects."

So they come up with generic names like Paper Master. "What does a name like Xerox mean anyhow? Nothing. A name like Paper Master, on the other hand, helps us communicate the benefits of a better copier."

Even worse, they introduce the new brand as a line extension. "Nobody has ever heard of Xerox, a name that somebody just invented. On the other hand our firm, the Haloid Company, was founded in 1906. We have thousands of customers and a good reputation. Let's call our new plain-paper copier the Haloid Paper Master."

"Well," you might be thinking, "I would never make a mistake like that. I would never call a new product with as much potential as the 914 copier had the 'Haloid Paper Master.'"

In retrospect, no. In futurespect, maybe you would. At least the vast majority of the companies we have worked with almost always prefer line-extended generic names to unique new brand names.

On a global scale, this is the biggest issue in the business community. Companies are divided into two camps: those who believe that the essence of business success is in the continuing development of superior products and services and those who believe in branding. The product versus the brand.

The product camp dominates the marketing scene. "The brand name doesn't matter. What counts is how the product performs."

As proof of this principle, product campers are quick to reduce the argument to absurdity. "If the product is no good, the product will fail regardless of whether the product has a good brand name or not."

Is a Xerox copier better than a Canon copier? How does a Ricoh copier compare with a Sharp copier?

Have you ever bought a copier? Which brand of copier is no good? Forget copiers. Which brands of any products are no good?

Sure, some people will dump on some brands. They might even say things like "I'd never buy a Jaguar." But these opinions are seldom universal.

The no-good product is the red herring of marketing. It is constantly being used to justify the no-brand strategies of most companies.

We don't mean literally a no-brand strategy. A company might own brands that might be called brands from a legal point of view in the sense that their names are registered trademarks. But the company's strategies are based on building the better product or service, and the brands it uses to accompany these products have little power in the prospect's mind.

Product campers dominate the East Asia economy. Virtually every Asian company uses a megabrand, masterbrand, or line-extension strategy.

What's a Mitsubishi? Sixteen of the one hundred largest Japanese companies market products and services under the Mitsubishi name. Everything from automobiles to semiconductors to consumer electronics. From space equipment to transport systems.

What's a Matsushita? Same problem as Mitsubishi. Eight of the one hundred largest Japanese companies market products and services under the Matsushita name. Everything from electric equipment to electronic products and components. From batteries to refrigeration equipment.

What's a Mitsui? Same problem as Matsushita. Eight of the one hundred largest Japanese companies market products and services under the Mitsui name.

Compare Japan with the United States. The top hundred companies in the United States had sales last year of $2.8 trillion. As it happens, the top hundred companies in Japan also had sales last year of $2.8 trillion.

The real difference is in profits. The one hundred American companies had profits on average of 6.3 percent of sales. The one hundred Japanese companies had profits on average of just 1.1 percent of sales.

That 1.1 percent is the average net profit in Japan. With so many companies close to the break-even point, you can be sure that many are losing money on a regular basis.

The Asian practice of fielding a wide variety of products under the same brand name has drawn favorable comments from many business writers who don't always look under the financial covers to find the real story.

Korea is in even worse shape than Japan. Last year the twenty-five largest Korean companies made 0.8 percent net profit on sales.

Take Hyundai, for example. This $71 billion Korean *chaebol* brags about a "chips to ships" strategy. Hyundai makes microprocessors, telecommunications satellites, passenger cars, commercial vehicles, subways, high-speed trains, turnkey engineering and construction projects, supertankers, LNG carriers, among other products. All under the Hyundai name. Hyundai make everything, but they don't make very much money.

Throughout Asia you see the same pattern. Rampant line extensions that are destroying brands. (When you expand, you reduce the power of a brand. When you contract, you increase its power.)

Brands are not just something to think about at marketing meetings. Brands are the essence of the company itself. A company's very existence depends on building brands in the mind. And so does a country's.

East Asia does not have a banking problem, a financial problem, a monetary problem, or a political problem.

East Asia has a branding problem.

With a powerful marketing program, Miller High Life was rapidly gaining on market leader Budweiser. (It got within 20 percent of the King of Beers.) Then Miller introduced a bevy of line-extension brands and stopped Miller High Life cold.

10
The Law of Extensions

*The easiest way to destroy a brand is
to put its name on everything.*

You don't have to go to Asia to find examples of rampant
line extension.

More than 90 percent of all new products introduced in
the U.S. grocery and drug trade are line extensions.
Which is the major reason that stores are choked with
brands. (There are 1,300 shampoos, 200 cereals, 250 soft
drinks.)

Scanner data indicates that many of those line extensions (at least in supermarkets) sit on the shelf and gather
dust. Research from Kroger supermarkets in Columbus,
Ohio, found that of the average 23,000 items in a store,
6,700 sold in a day, 13,600 sold in a week, and 17,500 sold
in a month, leaving 5,500 that sold nothing in an entire
month.

This plethora of line extensions, in our opinion, is the reason for the increased demands from retailers for trade promotions, slotting fees, and return privileges.

According to industry experts, power has been shifting from manufacturers to retailers. The primary reason is line extension. With so many products to choose from, retailers can force manufacturers to pay for the privilege of getting their products on the shelf. If one company won't pay, the retailer can always find another company that will.

No industry is as line-extended as the beer industry. Before the launch of Miller Lite in the mid-seventies, there were three major beer brands: Budweiser, Miller High Life, and Coors Banquet.

Today these three brands have become sixteen: Budweiser, Bud Light, Bud Dry, Bud Ice, Miller Regular, Miller High Life, Miller Lite, Miller Genuine Draft, Miller Genuine Draft Light, Miller Regular, Miller Reserve, Miller Reserve Light, Miller Reserve Amber Ale, Coors, Coors Light, and Coors Extra Gold.

Have these sixteen brands increased their market share over that obtained by the original three brands? Not really. There has been some increase, but no greater than what you might expect. Big brands always put pressure on smaller brands, in the same way that Coke and Pepsi have eroded the market share of Royal Crown Cola.

Has the availability of these sixteen varieties of Budweiser, Miller, and Coors increased beer consumption? No. Per capita beer consumption over the past twenty-five years has been relatively flat. (Cola consumption in the same period of time has almost doubled.)

When your customers are not exactly rushing out to buy your product, why would you need more brands to satisfy those customers? Logic suggests you would need fewer brands.

But that's customer logic. Manufacturer logic is different. If volume is going nowhere, the manufacturer concludes it needs more brands to maintain or increase sales. When a category is increasing in sales, there are opportunities for new brands, but manufacturer logic suggests they're not needed. "We are doing great, we don't need any more brands."

As a result, the marketplace is filled with line extensions in areas where they are not needed and is starved for new brands in areas where they *are* needed. Figure that one out.

Another reason for the rise in line extensions is a company's natural instinct to copy the competition. Miller's introduction of Miller Lite was quickly followed by Schlitz Light, Coors Light, Bud Light, Busch Light, Michelob Light, and Pabst Light. The light list is endless.

It's painful to remember and so hard to forget. After the introduction of Miller Lite, we rushed around the brewing industry with a simple message: Keep your beer brand focused on the regular market. That will give you a leg up on Joe Sixpack, who consumes an awful lot of beer. (You can see how successful we were with our message.)

Why did Miller introduce Miller Regular, a brand which most beer drinkers have never heard of? Because Anheuser-Busch has regular Budweiser, Coors has regular Coors, and Miller didn't have a regular beer.

Don't laugh. This is the way companies think. The competition must know something we don't know. Let's do the same thing.

One reason 90 percent of all new brands are line extensions is that management measures results with the wrong end of the ruler. It measures only the success of the extension. It never measures the erosion of the core brand.

And it's not just the erosion, it's also the lost opportunities. Big powerful brands should have market shares approaching 50 percent, like Coca-Cola, Heinz, Pop-Tarts, Jell-O, and Gerber's. But it's hard to find more than a few such brands. Most big brands have been line-extended to death.

- Budweiser (all varieties combined) has less than 30 percent of the beer market.
- Marlboro (a brand that comes in at least a dozen different varieties, including Marlboro Lights, Marlboro Medium, and Marlboro Menthol) has only 30 percent of the cigarette market.

- IBM has only 10 percent of the personal computer market.

When Coors was planning the introduction of Coors Light, we asked one of its executives, "Where is the Coors Light business going to come from?"

"Oh, we're going to take it away from Budweiser and Miller."

When Budweiser was planning the introduction of Bud Light, the targets were Miller and Coors.

When Miller was planning the introduction of Miller Lite, the targets were Budweiser and Coors.

Maybe this concept is too complicated for the average CEO to understand, but isn't the Coors Light drinker more likely to come from Coors? And the Bud Light drinker from Budweiser? And the Miller Lite drinker from Miller High Life?

Certainly the numbers substantiate this conclusion. Since the introduction of the three lights, the three regular beer brands have all declined substantially.

(And what can you say about Coors Rocky Mountain Spring Water? Born in 1990. Died in 1992. Mourned by no one. Not too many beer drinkers wanted to shift from beer to water.)

The market, you might be thinking, is shifting from regular to light beer. That's true. But it's really two markets and the best way to capture those two markets is with two brands.

But there are no beer brands that are not line-extended, you might have concluded. And you're right. And what a wonderful opportunity for someone who understands the laws of branding.

Actually, until a short time ago, there was one: Amstel Light, which became the leading brand of imported light beer. So what did Heineken USA, the importer of Amstel Light, do next? It introduced Amstel Bier (regular beer) and Amstel 1870 beer.

Who drinks Diet Coke and Diet Pepsi? Do you really suppose that these diet drinkers used to drink beer, ginger ale, or orange juice? We don't.

Diet Coke comes out of Coca-Cola's hide. Sure, the diet cola market has boomed, thanks to the public's interest in low-calorie products. But what Coca-Cola should have done is to launch a second brand.

Actually it did. After the success of Diet Pepsi, Coca-Cola launched Tab. And Tab was doing quite well. The day Diet Coke was introduced, Tab was leading Diet Pepsi in market share by about 32 percent.

Now which is the better name: Diet Pepsi or Tab? If line extension is the superior way to build a brand, why did Tab lead Diet Pepsi by nearly a third?

Of course, Coke nearly killed Tab by keeping Nutrasweet out of the brand and only putting it into Diet Coke. But you can't squeeze a good idea out of the marketplace. Tab still hangs in there with almost no promotional support.

When the low-fat craze hit the cookie market, almost every brand rushed out with a line-extended version of its regular cookie. As a matter of fact, the first fat-free cookie and early leader was Fat Free Fig Newtons.

Nabisco took a different approach. Instead of launching a line extension, it launched a new brand called Snack-Well's. Fat Free Fig Newtons were only a modest success, while SnackWell's became the eighth-largest-selling grocery item, right behind Diet Coke.

So what did SnackWell's do next? You already know the answer to that question. Put its name on everything except the kitchen sink. Prognosis: SnackWell's will do poorly in the future.

The issue is clear. It's the difference between building brands and milking brands. Most managers want to milk. "How far can we extend the brand? Let's spend some serious research money and find out."

Sterling Drug was a big advertiser and a big buyer of research. Its big brand was Bayer aspirin, but aspirin was losing out to acetaminophen (Tylenol) and ibuprofen (Advil).

So Sterling launched a $116-million advertising and marketing program to introduce a selection of five "aspirin-free" products. The Bayer Select line included headache-pain relief, regular pain relief, nighttime pain relief, sinus-pain relief, and a menstrual relief formulation, all of which contained either acetaminophen or ibuprofen as the core ingredient.

Results were painful. The first year Bayer Select sold
$26 million worth of pain relievers in a $2.5 billion market, or about 1 percent of the market. Even worse, the
sales of regular Bayer aspirin kept falling at about 10 percent a year. Why buy Bayer aspirin, if the manufacturer is
telling you that its "select" products are better because
they are "aspirin-free"?

Are consumers stupid or not?

Many manufacturers are their own worst enemies.
What are line extensions like *light, clear, healthy,* and *fat-
free* actually telling you? That the regular products are not
good for you.

- Heinz Light ketchup? Don't you suppose this leads
  customers to draw the conclusion that ketchup is
  loaded with calories? (Today, salsa outsells ketchup. As
  night follows day, we are sure to see in the future a
  brand called Pace Light salsa.)
- Hellmann's Light mayonnaise? Same question.
- Campbell's Healthy Request soup? Regular soup is
  unhealthy?
- Crystal Pepsi? What is wrong with the color of regular
  Pepsi?

Should Evian launch Sulfate-Free Evian spring water?
(Check the label, there are 10 mg of sulfates in a liter of
regular Evian. There are probably people out there who
would like a sulfate-free version.)

The Law of Extensions

Let sleeping brands lie. Before you launch your next line extension, ask yourself what customers of your current brand will think when they see the line extension.

If the market is moving out from under you, stay where you are and launch a second brand. If it's not, stay where you are and continue building your brand.

One of the best locations for a number-two brand is across the street from the leader. The best place for a Planet Hollywood is right across the street from its biggest competitor, Hard Rock Cafe. Both brands will benefit.

11

The Law of Fellowship

In order to build the category, a brand
should welcome other brands.

Greed often gets in the way of common sense. The
dominant brand in a category often tries to broaden
its appeal in order to capture every last bit of market
share.

"If we served beer and wine," the CEO of McDonald's
once said, "we might eventually have 100 percent of the
food-service market."

Unlikely. The law of expansion suggests the opposite.
When you broaden your brand, you weaken it. Look what
happened when McDonald's tried to broaden its appeal to
the adult market with the Arch Deluxe sandwich. Its mar-

ket share fell and ultimately it was forced to discontinue the product.

Which brings us to the law of fellowship. Not only should the dominant brand tolerate competitors, it should welcome them. The best thing that happened to Coca-Cola was Pepsi-Cola. (To that end it's ironic that the Coca-Cola Company fought Pepsi-Cola in the courts over the use of "Cola" in its name. Fortunately for Coke, it lost, creating a category which has been growing like gangbusters ever since.)

Choice stimulates demand. The competition between Coke and Pepsi makes customers more cola conscious. Per capita consumption goes up.

Remember, customers have choices, even when there is no competition. They can choose to drink beer, water, ginger ale, or orange juice instead of a cola. Competition increases the noise level and tends to increase sales in the category.

Competition also broadens the category while allowing the brands to stay focused. If Coca-Cola appeals to older people and Pepsi-Cola to younger people, the two brands can stay focused (and powerful) while at the same time broadening the market.

Customers respond to competition because choice is seen as a major benefit. If there is no choice, customers are suspicious. Maybe the category has some flaws? Maybe the price is too high? Who wants to buy a brand if you don't have another brand to compare it with?

You seldom see a big, growing, dynamic market without several major brands. Take the office superstore market. There are three big brands competing tooth and nail for this market: Office Depot, Office Max, and Staples.

So effective has this competition been that the number of independent office stationery stores has declined from about 10,000 in the past decade to 3,000 stores today.

Instead of welcoming competition, companies often feel threatened because they believe that future market shares will be based on the merits of the individual brands. An even playing field is not what most companies want. They want an unfair advantage, a playing field tilted to their side. Therefore, they think, let's try to drive out competitors before they get too established.

In the process, however, they fall victim to the laws of branding. Expansion, line extensions, and other strategies that broaden a brand's appeal will ultimately weaken the brand.

Market share is not based on merit, but on the power of the brand in the mind. In the long run, a brand is not necessarily a higher-quality product, but a higher-quality name. (See Chapter 9, "The Law of the Name.")

Of course, customers can have too much choice. The more brands, the more flavors, the more varieties, the more confusion in the category. And the lower the per capita consumption.

For each category, two major brands seem to be ideal. Coca-Cola and Pepsi-Cola in cola, for example. Listerine and Scope in mouthwash. Kodak and Fuji in photographic film. Nintendo and PlayStation in video games. Duracell and Energizer in appliance batteries.

When there is too much choice, consumption suffers. Take wine, for example. In California alone, there are more than 1,000 wineries and 5,000 brands. *Wine Spectator* magazine publishes an annual issue with rankings of some 24,000 individual wines. (If you drank a bottle a day, it would take you more than sixty-five years to run through the lot. Then you would probably be too old to remember which wine you liked the best!)

With all that choice, you might think that Americans drink a lot of wine. But we don't. The per capita consumption of wine in the United States is one-tenth that of France and one-ninth that of Italy. Even the average German drinks three and a half times as much wine as the average American.

With so many small vineyards, so many different varieties, and a handful of connoisseurs with individual opinions about taste, the wine industry has yet to see the rise of any major brand. "That's just the way wine is," say industry experts. "Wine needs multiple brands, multiple vintages, multiple varieties." The motto seems to be "every acre its own brand."

That might be the law of wine, but it's not the law of

branding. One day some company will do in wine what Absolut did in vodka and Jack Daniel's did in whiskey: build a big, powerful, worldwide brand.

You can also see the law of fellowship at work in the retail arena. Where one store may not make it, several stores will. Instead of being spread out in every section of a city, used-car dealers are often clustered along "automotive row." Where one dealer might have had trouble surviving, a handful of dealers are prospering. That's the power of fellowship.

In any large city, you can see the same law in action. Similar businesses tend to congregate in the same neighborhood. In New York City, for example, you will find the garment district on Seventh Avenue, the financial district on Wall Street, the diamond district on Forty-seventh Street, advertising agencies on Madison Avenue, theaters on Broadway, theme restaurants on West Fifty-seventh Street, art galleries in SoHo, and peep shows on Forty-second Street (although Mayor Giuliani is trying to move them elsewhere).

It makes sense for similar businesses to be located close together. First, a group of similar businesses attract more customers to an area because there is more than one store to shop at. Second, customers can easily comparison shop among stores. Customers feel that without competition, companies may take advantage of them and rip them off. (The airlines have a reputation for doing this.) Third, having the competition nearby allows companies to keep an eye on each other. Companies are always anxious to keep track of trends in their industries.

Planet Hollywood discovered that one of the best locations in a city for its restaurant was across the street from its arch rival, Hard Rock Cafe. People attracted to this type of theme restaurant are already drawn to the area thanks to Hard Rock and can easily be enticed to eat at a Planet Hollywood across the street. Similarly, the best location for a Burger King franchise is often across the street from a McDonald's restaurant.

Take Branson, Missouri, which bills itself as the "music show capital of the world." Where one music theater in a town of 3,706 people might be hard-pressed to make ends meet, forty music theaters are well and prospering. It's the power of fellowship.

Your brand should welcome healthy competition. It often brings more customers into the category.

And remember, no brand can ever own the entire market (unless of course it is a government-sanctioned monopoly).

Realistically, how much market share can the dominant brand achieve? Our research indicates that 50 percent is about the upper limit.

Federal Express has a 45 percent share of the domestic overnight package delivery market. Coca-Cola has a 50 percent share of the domestic cola market. For market shares higher than 50 percent, you need to consider launching multiple brands. Not just line extensions, but separate individual brands. (See Chapter 15, "The Law of Siblings.")

Blockbuster Video is a good brand name for a video rental store, while General Video Rental is not. Brands should avoid generic names like the plague. Yet wherever you look, you see a raft of generic names, especially in the retail area.

12

The Law of the Generic

One of the fastest routes to failure is giving a brand a generic name.

History often leads us astray. In the past, some of the most successful companies (and brands) had generic names.

- General Motors, General Electric, General Mills, General Foods, General Dynamics.
- Standard Oil, Standard Brands, Standard Register Company, Standard Products Company.
- American Airlines, American Motors, American Broadcasting Company, American Telephone & Telegraph, American Express, Aluminum Company of America.
- National Broadcasting Company, National Biscuit Company, National Car Rental.
- International Business Machines, International Paper, International Harvester, International Nickel.

Some companies have even tried to combine two or more of these lofty "all things to all people" names. The American General Life and Accident Insurance Company, for example. We're surprised that nobody thought to use "International General American Standard Products Company."

In the past, companies thought they needed big, scopy, generic names. And the brand name was almost always the company name. (Today such an approach might produce the General Global Corp.) And yet, this naming strategy clearly worked. Why?

Years ago the market was flooded with commodities produced by thousands of small companies operating in a single town or region. The big, scopy, generic names put these small competitors in their place.

Many of these General, Standard, American, National, and International companies are still operating (and are still successful) today. Some of them are among the largest and best-known brands in the world.

The fact is, these brands/companies are successful in spite of their names.

We believe the primary reason for these corporate successes is the strategy and not the name.

- National Biscuit Company was the first national biscuit company.
- General Electric was the first general electric company.
- International Harvester was the first international harvester company.

Being first in the marketplace gave these companies such a head start and such a powerful presence in the market that it overcame the liability of their generic names.

Witness the shift from generic (or general) names to specific names: Nabisco, Alcoa, NBC, GE, ABC, IBM.

There are many national biscuit companies, but only one Nabisco. There are many aluminum companies in America, but only one Alcoa. There are many national broadcasting companies, but only one NBC.

Of course, we're sure that NBC always considered itself the National Broadcasting Company rather than a "national broadcasting company."

And therein lies the biggest mistake made when picking brand names. The process proceeds visually rather than verbally.

Executives often pass around the boardroom logotypes of prospective brand names, set in type and mounted on foamcore.

But the vast majority of brand communication takes place verbally, not visually. The average person spends nine times as much time listening to radio and television than he or she does reading magazines and newspapers.

Furthermore, in order to give meaning to the printed word, the mind processes sounds. The printed word is secondary to the sound that it generates in the reader's mind. So how can a reader differentiate the word "general" from the word "General"? With great difficulty.

The problem with a generic brand name is its inability to differentiate the brand from the competition. In the food supplement field, for example, a brand called Nature's Resource is spending $5 million a year to break into this growing market.

On the shelves of your local GNC store you'll also find the following products:

- Nature's Answer.
- Nature's Bounty.
- Nature's Herb.
- Nature's Secret.
- Nature's Way.
- Nature's Best.
- Nature's Gate.
- Nature's Plus.
- Nature's Sunshine Products.
- Nature's Works.

Will any of these generic brands break into the mind and become a major brand? Unlikely.

Even the legendary Lee Iacocca, father of the Mustang and former CEO of Chrysler Corporation (two powerful name brands), took the generic road when he launched his own company, EV Global Motors. EV, for electric vehicle, is introducing a $995 electric bicycle. We can't see customers asking for an "EV Global bike."

What about a brand name, Lee? Like Schwinn or Trek or Cannondale?

The high-tech field is loaded with generic names that are unlikely to generate much in the way of brand identity. Security Software Systems, Power and Data Technology, Server Technology. Compare those names to Microsoft,

Compaq, and Intel and you can see the power of a meaningful brand name.

McAfee Associates, the leading maker of antivirus software, recently bought Network General for $1.3 billion. Guess what it chose for a new name?

It dropped McAfee, the only "name, name" it owned in favor of two generics: Network Associates. It knew it had a name problem so it is spending $10 million on the company's first television campaign, including more than a million for a Super Bowl spot.

As those thirty seconds flew by, did the viewer hear the words "network associates" or "Network Associates"? Generic names disappear into the ether. Only brand names register in the mind.

Just for Men hair coloring is also spending a fortune trying to build its brand. After watching a television commercial, the gray-haired man might think to himself, "What is the name of that hair-coloring product that's just for men?"

Nobody is saying that you should always invent a new name for an established brand, although that's often a good strategy for a product or service that is truly revolutionary and unlikely to be copied for some time. Kodak and Xerox are the usual suspects.

What you should generally do is to find a regular word taken out of context and used to connote the primary attribute of your brand.

Blockbuster Video is a powerful brand name. General Video Rental is not.

Hollywood brags about its "blockbusters," so Blockbuster Video borrowed the term to suggest it rents the best movies.

Budget is a powerful brand name for a car-rental service. The word suggests that it rents cars at low prices. Low-Cost Car Rental is not a good brand name.

Service Merchandise is a $4 billion company with a General Video name. It's too bad. The company's concept is compelling, but its generic name dooms the brand to relative obscurity.

The Luxury Car Company would have gone nowhere, in our opinion, but Toyota took the word "luxury," tweaked a few letters, and came up with Lexus, a superb brand name for a Japanese luxury car.

Some genius took the name of a specific office product and used it out of context to come up with Staples, an effective brand name for an office supplies company. The double-entendre is particularly powerful. "Buy your office staples from Staples."

Sometimes you can carve out a brand name by cutting a generic in half. This often has the further advantage of creating a short, distinctive, easy-to-remember brand name. Intelligent Chip Company is a lousy brand name, but Intel Corp. is terrific.

"Intelligent Chip inside" is a lousy advertising slogan. All computers have intelligent chips inside, but only the top-of-the-line products have "Intel inside."

One reason that line extensions fare so poorly in the

marketplace is that they generally combine a brand name with a generic name. The weak generic name fails to create the separate identity that is the essence of the branding process. "Michelob Light" is perceived in the mind as "Michelob light," a watered-down version of the regular beer.

The mind doesn't deal in letters. It deals in sounds. You can capitalize all you want, but a generic word is a generic word in the mind, no matter how you spell it.

Sometimes a company gets lucky. The line extension Vaseline Intensive Care skin lotion became the number-one hand lotion brand because the customer inadvertently treated Intensive Care as a brand name, not a descriptive generic name.

How do we know this to be true? Because customers call the product Intensive Care. "Hand me the Intensive Care."

Customers don't say, "Hand me the Vaseline." Unless, of course, they want the Vaseline.

On the other hand, if Vaseline had followed conventional line-extension thinking, it would have called the brand Vaseline Heavy-Duty skin lotion. "Hand me the Heavy Duty" is not something people are likely to say.

So why didn't Chesebrough-Pond's just call the brand Intensive Care in the first place? Good question and good thinking. You're ready for the next law.

Does the Tide brand need the corporate endorsement of the company name, Procter & Gamble? Probably not. Will a corporate endorsement hurt the brand? Probably not. Corporate endorsements are primarily for the trade, not for the enlightenment of the consumer.

13
The Law of the Company

Brands are brands. Companies are companies. There is a difference.

Nothing causes as much confusion in the branding process as the proper use of a company name.

- Should the company name dominate the brand name?
  For example: Microsoft dominates Microsoft Word.
- Should the brand name dominate the company name?
  For example: Tide dominates Procter & Gamble.
- Or should they be given equal weight?
  For example: Gillette Sensor.

The issue of how to use a company name is at the same time both simple and complicated. Simple, because the laws are so clear-cut. Complicated, because most companies do not follow the simple laws of branding and end up with a system that defies logic and results in endless brand versus company debates.

Brand names should almost always take precedence over company names. Consumers buy brands, they don't buy companies. So when a company name is used alone as a brand name (GE, Coca-Cola, IBM, Xerox, Intel), customers see these names as brands.

When you combine a company name with a brand name in a clear and consistent fashion, the brand name is the primary name and the company name is seen as the secondary name: General Motors Cadillac.

Simple observation will demonstrate how seldom customers will use a company name . . . when they have been given a viable brand name to use. "How do you like my new Cadillac?"

Nobody says, "How do you like my new General Motors luxury car?"

With this caveat in mind, a company is a company as long as the name is not being used as a brand. A brand is a brand. There is a difference. A company is the organization that manufactures or produces the brand. It is not the brand itself. Microsoft isn't Word, Procter & Gamble isn't Tide. Microsoft produces many products, one of which is Word. Procter & Gamble produces many products, one of which is Tide.

While this makes sense, it's not usually the best branding strategy. Unless there are compelling reasons to do otherwise, the best branding strategy should be to use the company name as the brand name.

The WD-40 Company produces the WD-40 brand. The Zippo Corporation produces the Zippo brand. The Coca-Cola Company produces the Coca-Cola brand. Neat, simple, straightforward, easy to understand.

1. What's a Coca-Cola?
2. What's a Zippo?
3. What's a WD-40?

When you are a customer or prospect, the instant answers that come to mind are:

1. Cola.
2. Windproof lighter.
3. Lubricating spray.

When you are an employee of Coca-Cola, Zippo, or WD-40, on the other hand, the answer is usually different. It's the name on the paycheck. It's "my company."

Managers are employees, too. That's why management is company-oriented. And customers are brand-oriented.

Does the consumer care whether Toyota, Honda, or Nissan makes the Lexus? Probably not. But the president of Toyota USA certainly cares.

Does the customer care whether Nabisco or Kraft or General Foods makes Oreo cookies? Probably not. But the Nabisco marketing manager handling the Oreo brand certainly does.

Do you really care whether the publisher of this book was HarperBusiness, Simon & Schuster, or McGraw-Hill? (Do you even know without looking at the spine?)

But Laureen Connelly Rowland does. (She is our editor at HarperBusiness. And a good one, too.)

The view from the inside is totally different than the view from the outside. Managers must constantly remind themselves that customers care only about brands, not about companies.

It goes deeper than that. The brand isn't just the name the manufacturer puts on the package. It's the product itself. To a customer, Coca-Cola is, first and foremost, a dark, sweet, reddish-brown liquid. The brand name is the word customers use to describe that liquid. What's inside the bottle is the most important aspect of the branding process. Coca-Cola is branding the liquid itself.

It's not a cola made by the Coca-Cola Company. The cola itself is Coca-Cola, the real thing. This distinction is at the heart of an effective branding strategy.

A company that truly understands branding from the customer's point of view would have never introduced a product called "New Coke." How can you have a new, presumably better Coke? How can the real thing have been bad? Why on earth would you ever change it? It's like introducing a New God.

In the same way, Rolex is not the brand name of an

expensive sports watch made by the Rolex Watch Company Ltd. A Rolex is what you wrap around your wrist.

- Pop-Tarts are what you put in the toaster.
- Band-Aids are what you put on cuts.
- Tylenol is what you take for headaches.

Most issues involving company names versus brand names can be solved by asking yourself two questions:

1. What is the name of the brand?
2. What is the name of the stuff inside the packaging?

Both names had better be the same or you have big problems.

Let's explore what happens when you use both the company name and the brand name on the package. Let's look at Microsoft Excel.

The "Microsoft" part of the name is redundant. Nobody but Microsoft makes Excel software. Since customers tend to simplify names as much as possible, Microsoft Excel quickly becomes Excel. "Let's buy Excel."

Microsoft Word is another matter. "Word" is a generic word. Furthermore, many of Microsoft's competitors have used "word" in their product names. WordPerfect, WordStar, etc. As a result, customers tend to use the full name of the product, "Microsoft Word." This is not necessarily good from the company's point of view. As a general rule, you want your brand name to be as short and as memorable as possible. (Short names greatly improve your word-of-mouth possibilities.)

When customers feel they have to use both your company name and your brand name together, you usually have a branding problem. (Normally because you used a generic word for your brand name.) Take Campbell's Chunky soup, for example.

Is the product Chunky soup or chunky soup? Customers can't be sure, so they ask for Campbell's Chunky soup. Campbell should have used a different brand name.

Take the Sony Trinitron. Is trinitron a type of cathode-ray tube or is Trinitron a brand name for a television set? Customers aren't sure, so they ask for a Sony Trinitron.

As far as the customer is concerned, the easiest, simplest way is the Procter & Gamble way. Use just the brand name boldly on the package and relegate "The Procter & Gamble Company" to tiny type at the bottom. That's how the company name is handled on Bold, Cheer, Ivory, Tide, etc.

But a case can be made for the middle way. Some of today's more sophisticated, discriminating customers might like to know who makes a particular brand. They won't, however, use both names together. Nobody calls an Acura a "Honda Acura." Or a Lincoln a "Ford Lincoln."

Furthermore, there is often interest in the trade (which includes retailers and distributors) about the company behind a brand. For example, where do we order Tide from?

For many brands one answer is to put the company name in small type above the brand name. Customers who are strongly motivated to use only the brand name will hardly notice the company name. Yet the trade and today's more sophisticated customers will be able to easily find the name of the company behind the brand.

The danger, of course, lies inside the corporation. With this branding strategy, you tend to get inundated with suggestions like, "Why can't we make the corporate name larger? We're wasting all these opportunities to promote our stock, improve employee relationships, build a better relationship with the trade." (On second thought, maybe you should leave the company name off the brand entirely.)

Look what happened at Gillette. Both the Trac II and the Atra razors were introduced with a small "Gillette" above the brand names.

Then along came the Sensor and the company decided to set the name "Gillette" in the same size as "Sensor." Not a good idea. The brand name should dominate the company name.

With the Mach 3, Gillette has returned to basics. The Mach 3 name dominates.

No issue in branding is so thoroughly discussed as the proper role and function of the company name. And yet, in most cases, it's a non-issue.

The brand itself should be the focus of your attention. If you have to use the company name, use it. But do so in a decidedly secondary way.

❋ Holiday Inn

Holiday Inn has become a megabrand with the launch of subbrands like Holiday Inn Express, Holiday Inn Select, Holiday Inn SunSpree Resorts, and Holiday Inn Garden Court. This subbranding is eroding the power of the core brand.

14
The Law of Subbrands

What branding builds, subbranding
can destroy.

Management tends to invent terminology in order to give legitimacy to the branding moves it wants to make.

- Holiday Inn, the leading hotel/motel operator, wanted to get into the upscale hotel segment.
- Cadillac, the leading upscale domestic automobile manufacturer, wanted to introduce a smaller car.
- Waterford, the leading Irish crystal maker, wanted to market a less expensive line.
- Donna Karan, a top designer, wanted to market less costly and more casual clothes.

Typical line-extension strategies would have produced brand names like Holiday Inn Deluxe, Cadillac Light, Budget Waterford, and Kasual Karan. Even the most callow marketing people would have found these brand names difficult to swallow.

What to do? Invent a subbrand. So we have Holiday Inn Crowne Plaza, Cadillac Cimarron, Marquis by Waterford, and DKNY. Now we can have our cake and eat it, too. We can use our well-known core brand at the same time as we launch secondary or subbrands to move into new territory.

But what sounds right in the boardroom often doesn't make sense in the marketplace.

- Did anybody ever walk into a Holiday Inn and ask the clerk at the front desk: "Don't you have a more expensive hotel I can stay at?"
- Did anybody ever walk into a Cadillac dealership and ask: "Don't you have any smaller Cadillacs?" (Bigger maybe, but not smaller.)
- Did anybody ever walk into Bloomingdale's and ask the salesperson: "Don't you have any cheap Waterford?"
- Did anybody ever walk into a Donna Karan showroom and ask: "The suits are lovely, but where can I buy her sweatpants?"

The marketing world is awash in conceptual thinking that has no relationship to the real world. Subbranding is one of those concepts.

Customer research at Holiday Inn Crowne Plaza produced what you might have expected: "It's a nice hotel, but it's a little expensive for a Holiday Inn." The company finally got the message and is in the process of cutting the corporate connection. From now on, the hotels will be known as Crowne Plaza, period.

A Cadillac dealership is the last place in the world where you would look for a small car. The Cimarron went nowhere and was eventually dropped. Naturally, Cadillac didn't give up. Its latest small-car incarnation is called the Cadillac Catera.

On the other hand, Marquis by Waterford is a big success, but partially at the expense of the high-priced line. You have to wonder if there is a Gresham's law of marketing, too. Sooner or later, we expect the Marquis line to seriously erode the regular Waterford product.

Donna Karan has gone off in way too many directions. In addition to the basic line, there is Donna Karan menswear, DKNY, DKNY menswear, and DKNY kids. The company has also gotten into intimate apparel and beauty products. Recent financial reports have been poor.

Customers have a cornucopia of choice. Subbranders assume otherwise. Why would a customer expect Holiday Inn to have an upscale hotel? Wouldn't the customer more likely try Hilton, Hyatt, or Marriott first? Why spend all that money and still stay at a Holiday Inn! The thinking is, If I am forking out the big bucks, I want to stay with a top hotel brand.

Subbranding is an inside-out branding strategy that tries to push the core brand into new directions. It captures management's attention because of what it promises, not necessarily because of what it delivers.

In spite of the subbranding setback at Holiday Inn Crowne Plaza, the company has moved into Holiday Inn Express, Holiday Inn Select, Holiday Inn SunSpree Resorts, and Holiday Inn Garden Court.

You used to know exactly what you would find in a Holiday Inn. In fact, that was the theme of its long-running advertising campaign: "The best surprise is no surprise."

What's a Holiday Inn Select? Go ahead. Book a room and be surprised.

Subbranding has taken its share of criticism, so the marketing establishment is rethinking the concept. Leading-edge practitioners today are more likely to call the concept a masterbrand or megabrand strategy. It's especially prevalent in the automotive field.

"Ford is not our brand. Our brands are: Aspire, Contour, Crown Victoria, Escort, Mustang, Probe, Taurus, and Thunderbird." What's a Ford then? "A Ford is a megabrand."

"Dodge is not our brand. Our brands are: Avenger, Intrepid, Neon Stealth, Stratus, and Viper." What's a Dodge then? "A Dodge is a megabrand."

You can't apply your own branding system to a market that sees things differently. What the manufacturer sees as a brand, the customer sees as a model. What the manufacturer sees as a megabrand, the customer sees as a brand. (Customers don't understand the megabrand concept at all.)

Even Keith Crain, publisher of *Automotive News,* the industry's bible, is dubious of what car marketing people are trying to do. "A lot of folks out there tell you that individual models, not the nameplates, are the brands. I don't know of any models that have ads in the Yellow Pages."

Can a brand be marketed in more than one model? Sure, as long as those models don't detract from the essence of the brand, that singular idea or concept that sets it apart from all other brands. When you feel the need to create subbrands, you are chasing the market, you are not building the brand.

The essence of a brand is some idea or attribute or market segment you can own in the mind. Subbranding is a concept that takes the brand in exactly the opposite direction. Subbranding destroys what branding builds.

Branding concepts that are not driven by the marketplace are going to go nowhere. Subbranding, masterbranding, and megabranding are not customer-driven concepts. They have no meaning in the minds of most consumers.

Think simple. Think like a customer and your brand will become more successful.

ACURA

When Honda wanted to introduce an expensive car, it didn't call the brand a Honda Plus or a Honda Ultra. It developed a new brand called Acura, which became a big success. As a matter of fact, Acura quickly became the largest-selling imported luxury car in America.

15

The Law of Siblings

*There is a time and a place to launch
a second brand.*

The laws of branding seem to suggest that a company concentrate all of its resources on a single brand for a single market. Keep the brand focused and ignore opportunities to get into new territories.

True. But there comes a time when a company should launch a second brand. And perhaps a third, even a fourth brand.

A second-brand strategy is not for every company. If handled incorrectly, the second brand can dilute the power of the first brand, and waste resources. (See Chapter 10, "The Law of Extensions.")

Yet, in some situations, a family of brands can be developed that will assure a company's control of a market for many decades to come.

Take the Wm. Wrigley Jr. Company. For more than a hundred years, Wrigley has dominated the chewing gum market, generating billions of dollars of profits. But not with one brand. Today Wrigley has a family of brands.

- Big Red (a cinnamon-flavored brand).

- Doublemint (a peppermint-flavored brand).

- Extra (a sugar-free brand).

- Freedent (a stick-free brand).

- Juicy Fruit (a fruit-flavored brand).

- Spearmint (a spearmint-flavored brand).

- Winterfresh (a breath-freshener brand).

The key to a family approach is to make each sibling a unique individual brand with its own identity. Resist the urge to give the brands a family look or a family identity. You want to make each brand as different and distinct as possible.

The Wrigley approach is not perfect. Wrigley's first three brands (Juicy Fruit, Spearmint, and Doublemint) are too much like line extensions. They need the Wrigley name to support their generic brand names. Big Red, Extra, Freedent, and Winterfresh, however, can stand on their own, each as totally separate brands.

Most managers are too internally focused to see the power of a separate identity. They want to "take advantage of the equity" their brand already owns in the mind in order to successfully launch a new brand.

So IBM launches brands like the IBM PCjr. And NyQuil launches DayQuil. And Blockbuster Video launches Blockbuster Music. And Toys "R" Us launches Babies "R" Us.

Time Inc. became the world's largest magazine publisher, not by launching line extensions of its core brand, but by launching totally separate publications. Like Wrigley, Time Inc. has seven publishing powerhouses.

1. *Time.*

2. *Fortune.* (Not *Time for Business.*)

3. *Life.* (Not *Time for Pictures.*)

4. *Sports Illustrated.* (Not *Time for Sports.*)

5. *Money.* (Not *Time for Finances.*)

6. *People.* (Not *Time for Celebrities.*)

7. *Entertainment Weekly.* (Not *Time for Entertainment.*)

(Nobody's perfect. So now we also have *Digital Time, Teen People,* and *Sports Illustrated for Kids*.)

And what about *ESPN Magazine?* Does anyone except Disney really believe that *ESPN Magazine* will score any goals against *Sports Illustrated?* We certainly don't. The strength of a brand lies in having a separate, unique identity—not in being associated in the mind with a totally different category.

Having a totally separate identity in the mind doesn't mean creating a totally separate organization to handle each brand. Wm. Wrigley Jr. Company doesn't have seven separate manufacturing plants or seven separate sales organizations. It has seven brands and one company, one sales force, one marketing organization.

When General Mills decided to get into the Italian restaurant business, it didn't start from scratch. It used everything it learned about the seafood restaurant business to jump-start its Italian sibling. The one thing it did not do was to spin off its Red Lobster name. No Italian Red Lobsters.

General Mills invented a separate brand called Olive Garden. With this strategy, the company was able to create the two largest family restaurant chains in America. (Subsequently, the two chains were spun off into Darden

Restaurants, Inc., which immediately became the world's largest casual-dining company.)

When Sara Lee tried to take its panty hose brand into the supermarket trade, it didn't use its Hanes name. Nor did it call the new brand Hanes II or Hanes Too.

Sara Lee created a separate brand designed for supermarkets called L'eggs. Packaged in a plastic egg, the product became the number-one supermarket brand and the number-one panty hose brand, with 25 percent of the total panty hose market.

When Black & Decker, the world's largest power-tool manufacturer, wanted to get into the professional power-tool market, it didn't use the Black & Decker name. Nor did it call the new product Black & Decker Pro.

Black & Decker created a separate brand called DeWalt. In less than three years, DeWalt became a $350 million business, the market leader in professional tools and the second-largest power-tool brand after Black & Decker.

In the past, companies have created families of brands based on the principles behind the law of siblings. As time goes by, they forget why the brands were created in the first place. Instead of maintaining separate identities, the brands are mashed together and a layer of corporate frosting added on top. Instead of becoming stronger, the brands become weaker.

General Motors used to market a phalanx of five

brands, each with its own identity. Chevrolet, Pontiac, Oldsmobile, Buick, and Cadillac. Any twelve-year-old kid could spot a Chevy a block away and instantly identify the brand. Or a Pontiac. Or an Oldsmobile. Or a Buick. Or a Cadillac.

Holes in the front fender? That's a Buick. Fins on the back fenders? That's a Cadillac.

No more. Even if you work for General Motors, we defy you to spot GM cars on the street and then correctly identify the brands.

Many CEOs believe that a sibling strategy works best when the organization itself is decentralized. "Let the brands fight it out among themselves."

Not so. That belief is what got General Motors in trouble. Control over the brands (or divisions) was lifted and each division allowed to set its own course. Results were predictable. Each division broadened the scope of its brand and the world ended up with expensive Chevrolets, cheap Cadillacs, and bewildering brand confusion.

A sibling strategy requires more top-management supervision, not less. The urgent, long-term need is to maintain the separation between the brands, not to make them all alike. Human instincts work in the opposite direction. Result: All General Motors cars ended up with fins.

Nor is there a need to tag the corporate identity on every brand. Does the customer buy a Lexus because it's made by Toyota? Or in spite of the fact that it's made by Toyota?

The customer buys a Lexus. That's the power of the Lexus brand. The corporate connection is irrelevant.

In particular, corporate management should keep the following principles in mind when selecting a sibling strategy for its stable of brands.

1. Focus on a common product area. Passenger cars, chewing gum, over-the-counter drugs, these are some common product areas around which to build a sibling portfolio.

2. Select a single attribute to segment. Price is the most common, but other attributes include distribution, age, calories, sex, flavors. By segmenting a single attribute only, you reduce the potential confusion between your brands. What you want to avoid is any overlap among brands. Keep each brand unique and special.

3. Set up rigid distinctions among brands. Price is the easiest attribute to segment because you can put specific numbers on each brand. When prices overlap, it's very difficult to keep the brands separate. Most car owners confuse Oldsmobile and Buick because their price ranges are quite similar.

4. Create different, not similar brand names. You don't
   want to create a family of brands, you want to create a
   family of different brands. Look at some of Chevrolet's
   current model names: Cavalier, Camaro, Corsica,
   Caprice. One reason these model names can't be
   brands is the fact that they are too similar. If Chevrolet
   wanted to create brands instead of model names, it
   should have used distinctive names. Alliteration is the
   curse of a sibling family.

5. Launch a new sibling only when you can create a new
   category. New brands should not be launched just to
   fill a hole in the line or to compete directly with an
   existing competitor. This principle is the one most
   often violated by even the largest of companies. Coca-
   Cola launched Mr Pibb, not to create a new category,
   but to block the growth of Dr Pepper. Coca-Cola
   launched Fruitopia, not to create a new category, but to
   block the growth of Snapple. Both brands have gone
   nowhere.

6. Keep control of the sibling family at the highest level.
   If you don't, you will find that your powerful,
   distinctive brands will slowly fall apart. They will
   become victims of sibling rivalry, a pattern of corporate
   behavior that depends upon copying the best features
   of a brand's sibling competitors. You'll end up like

General Motors with a family of brands that all look alike.

A family of sibling brands is not a strategy for every corporation. But where it is appropriate, a sibling strategy can be used to dominate a category over the long term.

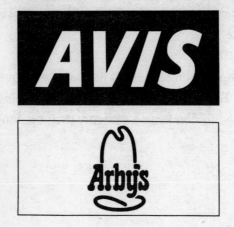

A customer sees the world through two
horizontally mounted eyes peering out of
his or her head. It's like looking out the
windshield of an automobile. For maximum
visual impact, a logotype should have the
same shape as a windshield, roughly two
and one-fourth units wide and one unit high.
The Avis logotype is almost the perfect shape.
The Arby's logotype is much too vertical.

16
The Law of Shape

*A brand's logotype should be designed
to fit the eyes. Both eyes.*

A logotype is a combination of a trademark, which is a visual symbol of the brand, and the name of the brand set in distinctive type.

Logotypes come in all shapes. Round, square, oval, horizontal, vertical. But all shapes are not created equal in the eyes of the consumer.

Since the eyes of your customers are mounted side by side, the ideal shape for a logotype is horizontal. Roughly two and one-fourth units wide and one unit high.

This horizontal shape will provide the maximum impact for your logotype. This is true wherever the logotype is used: on buildings, brochures, letterheads, advertisements, or calling cards.

This horizontal bias is especially important when a logotype is used on a retail establishment. In the neon jungle, a vertical logotype is at a severe disadvantage. The Arby's cowboy-hat logo is an example of the penalty of verticality.

Of equal importance to shape is legibility. Logotype designers often go way overboard in picking a typeface to express the attribute of a brand rather than its ability to be clearly read.

Typefaces come in thousands of styles and weights, but customers are only dimly aware of the differences. To paraphrase David Ogilvy, no woman says, I would have bought that detergent except they had to go and set the headline in Karnack Bold.

What typeface does Rolex use in its logotype? Ralph Lauren? Rolls-Royce? Serif or sans serif?

The truth is, the words (Rolex, Ralph Lauren, Rolls-Royce) are what communicate the power of the brands. The typefaces used in their logotypes can help or hinder the communication process, but only slightly.

On the other hand, if the typeface is virtually illegible, the logotype has little or no meaning in the consumer's mind. Not because of the typeface used, but because the prospect can't read the words. Legibility is the most important consideration in selecting a typeface used in a logotype.

Certainly, there are perceptual differences in the feelings that typefaces communicate. Sans serif typefaces look modern; serif typefaces look old-fashioned. Bold typefaces look masculine; light typefaces look feminine.

But these differences become obvious only by exaggeration. Would you really want to set your brand name in black-letter Gothic (the typeface used in the *New York Times* logotype) in order to make your brand look like an old, established brand? We think not. While it may make a visual impression, few prospects would be able to read (and therefore remember) the name.

It's a vicious cycle. In order to get the average prospect to notice the "mood" of the logotype you have to exaggerate the characteristics of the typography. And when you do that, you lose the logotype's legibility. It's not worth the trade-off.

The other component of the logotype, the trademark, or visual symbol, is also overrated. The meaning lies in the word, or words, not in the visual symbol.

It's the Nike name that gives meaning to the Swoosh symbol. The Swoosh symbol doesn't give much meaning to the Nike brand. After a symbol has been associated with a name for a long period of time, the symbol can represent the name, through a kind of "rebus" effect. But it's still the name that carries the brand's power.

So the Swoosh stands for Nike. But the advantages of using the symbol alone are slim and occur only in certain situations. Perhaps you can see the symbol at a distance where the name alone would be unreadable. Perhaps you can use the symbol on the product itself or on articles of

clothing where the name would look too "commercial."
Perhaps after spending more than $100 million a year for
over a decade to link the Swoosh to Nike, you can get
away with ending your commercials with only the symbol.
But what is the advantage in doing so?

Compare Shell with Mobil. Shell uses a shell trademark
on its gasoline stations without the word "Shell." Mobil
uses a logotype with blue letters and a red "O" to spell the
word "Mobil."

Is the Shell approach superior to the Mobil approach?
We think not. The best you can say is that the Shell
approach works, thanks to a simple name and an easy-to-
translate simple visual. But what are the advantages of the
Shell approach?

Very few. And there are some disadvantages. As people
grow up and new prospects come into the marketplace,
how will they learn that the yellow symbol means "Shell"?
Especially if the prospect doesn't know that Shell is a
brand name for a gasoline.

A great deal of effort has gone into creating elaborate
symbols for use in logotypes. Crests, shields, coats of
arms, and other heraldic symbols have poured out of
America's design shops in great profusion. For the most
part, these efforts are wasted. The power of a brand name
lies in the meaning of the word in the mind. For most
brands, a symbol has little or nothing to do with creating
this meaning in the mind.

The Law of Shape

There are only a handful of simple symbols that make effective trademarks. (The Mercedes three-pointed star is one of them.) At this late date, if history hasn't willed you one of these simple symbols, it's probably too late to create one on your own.

TIFFANY & CO.

What color is a Tiffany box? It's that distinctive robin's-egg blue. All Tiffany boxes are blue. If Tiffany had used a variety of colors for its boxes, it would have lost a marvelous opportunity to reinforce the brand name with a distinctive color.

17
The Law of Color

A brand should use a color that is the opposite of its major competitor's.

Another way to make a brand distinctive is with color. But color is not an easy attribute to work with. There are thousands of words to choose from in order to create a unique name, but only a handful of colors.

Basically there are five colors (red, orange, yellow, green, and blue) plus the neutral colors (black, white, and gray). It's best to stick to one of these five primary colors rather than an intermediate or mixed color. But which color?

Keep in mind that all colors are not created equal in the eye of the beholder. Colors on the red end of the spectrum are focused slightly in front of the retinas in your eyes. Therefore, a red color appears to move toward your eyes while you're looking at it.

Colors on the blue end of the spectrum, on the other hand, are focused slightly behind the retinas in your eyes. A blue color appears to move away from you.

Because of these physical reasons, red is the color of energy and excitement. Red is an in-your-face color. Which is why red is the dominant color in 45 percent of all national flags. (Blue is a distinct second. Blue dominates in less than 20 percent of all flags.)

Blue is the opposite of red. Blue is peaceful and tranquil. Blue is a laid-back color.

In the world of brands, red is a retail color used to attract attention. Blue is a corporate color used to communicate stability. For example, Coca-Cola red and IBM blue.

The other primary colors are in between. Orange is more like red than blue. Green is more like blue than red.

Yellow is the neutral color. But because it is in the middle of the range of wavelengths your eyes can detect, yellow is also the brightest color. (Its brightness is the reason yellow is often used to communicate "caution," as in yellow lights, yellow lines, yellow signs, etc.)

Over the years, some colors have become identified with various attributes, occasions, and movements.

- White is the color of purity (as in a white wedding gown).

- Black is the color of luxury (as in Johnnie Walker Black Label).

- Blue is the color of leadership (as in the blue ribbon award to the winner of a horse show).

- Purple is the color of royalty (as in the expression "born to the purple").

- Green is the color of the environment and health (as in Greenpeace, Healthy Choice, and SnackWell's).

When selecting a color for a brand or a logo, managers usually focus on the mood they want to establish rather than the unique identity they want to create. And while mood or tone can be important, other factors should override a choice based on mood alone.

Leaders have first choice. Normally the best color to select is the one that is most symbolic of the category. John Deere is the leading brand of farm tractor. Does it surprise you that John Deere picked green, the color of grass, trees, and agriculture, as the brand's signature color?

For a tractor company in Brazil, we were asked to

develop a brand name and color. We picked the name Maxion as the brand name because it seemed to communicate "power," a key attribute in a farm tractor. But what color should this new tractor brand use?

John Deere used green. The second brand in the market used red. So the color choice was obvious. Maxion became a blue tractor and a blue brand.

Is blue a good color for a farm tractor? No, but it's more important to create a separate brand identity than it is to use the right symbolic color.

Hertz, the first car-rental brand, picked yellow. So Avis, the second brand, picked red. National went with green. (For years, National gave out S&H Green Stamps to car-rental customers, a marketing move that helped associate the National name with the color green.)

There is a powerful logic for selecting a color that is the opposite of your major competitors. When you ignore this law of color, you do so at your own risk.

Cola is a reddish-brown liquid, so the logical color for a cola brand is red. Which is one reason why Coca-Cola has been using red for more than a hundred years.

Pepsi-Cola made a poor choice. It picked red and blue as the brand's colors. Red to symbolize cola and blue to differentiate the brand from Coca-Cola. For years Pepsi has struggled with a less-than-ideal response to Coke's color strategy.

Be honest. In your mind's eye, doesn't the world seem

to be awash in Coca-Cola signs? And isn't it hard to picture many Pepsi-Cola signs? Pepsi is out there, but the
lack of a unique differentiating color tends to make Pepsi
invisible in a sea of Coca-Cola red.

Recently Pepsi-Cola has seen the light, or rather the
color. It is doing what it should have done more than fifty
years ago. Make the brand's color the opposite of its major
competitors.

Pepsi-Cola is going blue. Pepsi even went to the
expense of painting a Concorde supersonic jet blue to
carry the color message to bottlers around the world.

Be the opposite. Kodak is yellow, so Fuji is green.

Yellow (as in the Golden Arches) is also the color most
identified with McDonald's, although the actual logotype
is mostly red. But what color is Burger King?

Burger King made the mistake of symbolizing the colors of a hamburger rather than picking a color to contrast
with the leaders. Burger King combined the yellow of a
hamburger bun with the orange-red of the meat. A neat
logotype, but a lousy color choice.

Budweiser is red, so what color should Miller be?

One of the many problems with the massive line extensions marketed by Miller is that they destroy the brand's
color identity. To differentiate the Miller line extensions
from each other, the brand uses an array of color combi-
nations. In the process Miller misses an opportunity to
differentiate its brand from Budweiser, its key competitor.

Think of the unmistakable color of a Tiffany box. By standardizing on a single color and using it consistently over the years, you can build a powerful visual presence in a clutter-filled world. At Christmastime, every brand and store uses green and red to celebrate the holiday, from M&M's to Macy's. Yet Tiffany & Co. sticks to blue, and becomes even more noticeable under the tree as a result.

Women hug their husbands as soon as they see the robin's-egg blue box—without opening it they know it will be wonderful.

You have probably seen many more Miller cans than Tiffany boxes, but we would bet that you know the hue of a Tiffany box and that you're not quite sure about Miller.

While a single color is almost always the best color strategy for a brand, sometimes you can make a case for multiple colors. Federal Express, the first overnight-package-delivery company, wanted its packages to stand out on the recipient's desk. So it combined the two most shocking colors it could find, orange and purple.

When a FedEx package arrives, everybody can see that a FedEx package has arrived. It's like an orange-and-purple suit in a sea of corporate blue.

Color consistency over the long term can help a brand burn its way into the mind. Look at what yellow has done for Caterpillar, brown for United Parcel Service, red for Coca-Cola, and blue for IBM.

What Big Blue did for IBM, a big color can do for your brand.

Heineken NV exports its brand to some 170 different countries. In most of these countries Heineken is the largest-selling high-priced beer. (Today Heineken brews its beer locally in some fifty countries.)

18

The Law of Borders

There are no barriers to global branding.
A brand should know no borders.

In our consulting work we find that most clients strongly believe two things:

1. Their brands' market shares cannot be substantially increased in their home countries.

2. They need to grow.

As a result of these ironclad beliefs, they insist on expanding their brands into other categories. "It's the only way to grow," they say.

So they fall victim to the first law of branding, the law of expansion. "Sure," they say. "Expanding our line may be dangerous, but it's the only way to grow."

It's not the only way to grow. In fact, the perfect solution to achieving both goals is to build a global brand. That means:

- Keep the brand's narrow focus in its home country.
- Go global.

For years the magic word on many products has been "imported." Food, beer, wine, liquor, clothing, automobiles, appliances, and many other items have benefited from an imported label. As if crossing a border suddenly increases the value of the brand.

Actually, crossing a border often does add value to a brand. Since value lies in the mind of the consumer, the perception of where the brand came from can add or subtract value. Does anyone doubt the value of:

- Watches from Switzerland.
- Wines from France.
- Automobiles from Germany.
- Electronic products from Japan.
- Clothing from Italy.

Would watches from Albania, wine from Poland, cars from Turkey, electronic products from Russia, or clothing from Portugal have the same perceptions? Obviously not.

Every country has its own unique perceptions. When a brand is in sync with its own country's perceptions, that brand has the possibility of becoming a global brand.

Wherever you live in the world today, chances are high that a significant number of people are wearing Swiss watches, driving German cars, drinking French wines, playing with Japanese electronic products, and dressing in Italian clothes. (Hopefully, not all at the same time.)

In spite of duties, tariffs, import quotas, inspections, regulations, red tape, and petty harassments, the world is becoming one big global market. And your product had better get on the global brandwagon or you risk losing out altogether.

Heineken NV is the leading brewery in the Netherlands, a small country with a population of only 15 million. Yet Heineken NV has become the second-largest brewery in the world by going global.

Can any brewery do the same? Of course not. To be successful as a worldwide beer brand (or any worldwide brand), you need to do two things:

1. You need to be first.
2. Your product needs to fit the perceptions of its country of origin.

Heineken was the first beer brand to pursue a global strategy. But beer is a product closely associated with Germany, not Holland.

Heineken got lucky. Holland is close to Germany, both geographically and ethnically. As a result, many beer drinkers think Heineken is a German product. (The company has been known to distribute cardboard coasters to bars and restaurants with the words "printed in Germany" featured on the coasters.)

Heineken got lucky in a second way. Beck's, its major German competitor on the global market, is saddled with an English-sounding name.

Heineken got lucky in a third way. The largest-selling German beer in Germany is Warsteiner. Normally, the leading brand in a country known for the category can be a big success in the rest of the world. (Witness the success of Barilla in the U.S. market with the theme "Italy's #1 pasta.") But no German beer brand starting with "War" is going to have much of a chance on the global beer market.

There are many ways to play the global game. Instead of appealing to the core market, you can appeal to a different segment of the market. Corona Extra has become a global force by associating the brand with the boom in Mexican cuisine. Kirin beer has done the same with Japanese cuisine. And Tsingtao beer with Chinese cuisine.

Corona Extra is a good example of the skillful use of a country's perception to promote a brand. Because a wedge of citrus was associated with the drinking of Mexican tequila, the importers of Corona Extra used the same imagery to launch the brand.

The toothpick and lime on top of the Corona bottle became a visual symbol that you could see halfway across a bar or restaurant. "What's that?" asked the non-Corona-drinking customer.

"It's Corona Extra, the Mexican beer." So successful was this strategy that the brand became the second-largest-selling imported beer in the United States after Heineken. In a twist, its American success has stimulated sales south of the border, where Corona Extra has become the leading beer brand in Mexico.

The perception of a country is important. There is no such thing as a global brand with a global perception.

- Toyota, Honda, and Nissan are global brands with Japanese perceptions.
- Compaq, Intel, and Microsoft are global brands with American perceptions.

- Dom Pérignon, Perrier-Jouët, and Château
  Mouton-Rothschild are global brands with French
  perceptions.
- Gucci, Versace, and Giorgio Armani are global brands
  with Italian perceptions.

With some 70 percent of its sales and 80 percent of its profits outside the United States, Coca-Cola insists that it is a global brand, not an American brand. And it is, literally. (Robert Goizueta, Coke's longtime chief executive, was from Cuba.)

But it would be a major marketing mistake for Coca-Cola to abandon its American heritage. Every brand (no matter where it is bottled, assembled, manufactured, or produced) has to be from somewhere. As American culture (especially in music, film, and television) has permeated the world, Coca-Cola has benefited greatly because of its American connection. "It's the real thing," Coke drinkers will say proudly with accents from places far and wide.

Every brand, just like every person, is from somewhere. A fifth-generation Irish-American might say he or she is "Irish." Coca-Cola, bottled in Mexico, is still a gringo brand. The same holds true for Levi's, the quintessential American brand.

It doesn't matter where your brand is conceived, designed, or produced, the name and its connotations determine its geographic perception. Häagen-Dazs might have been developed in New Jersey, but its origins sound Scandinavian.

A number of years ago we met with the chairman of the SMH Group, the company that makes the Swatch watch. "What would you think about an automobile made in Switzerland?" he asked.

"Great," we replied. "We have the perfect advertising headline: Runs like a watch."

"I'm glad you like the concept," he said. "We're going to call the new product the Swatch car."

"Wait a minute," we added. "Swatch is an inexpensive fashion watch you wear a few times and throw in the dresser drawer. An automobile is a serious product and a serious investment. People define themselves by what they drive. If you want to give your new car a watch name, call it a Rolex."

But he didn't listen. The company used the Swatch name while the car was under development (first in a joint venture with Volkswagen and then later with Mercedes-Benz). Recently, wiser heads prevailed and the name was changed to the Smart car.

Smart thinking. The Smart car will soon be available in Europe as a fuel-efficient, low-pollution car for congested cities.

The choice of the Smart name for a global product illustrates a trend in global branding: the use of English words for brands that may have no connection with the United Kingdom, the United States, Canada, Australia, or any other English-speaking country.

Take a new energy drink invented in Austria. The amino acid–infused, caffeine-injected, detoxifying, carbonated drink was not called *"Roter Stier."* Instead, the manufacturer used the English words "Red Bull."

Red Bull has become an "in" drink in Europe and is already starting to make inroads here in the United States.

The top three high-end brands of blue jeans ($100 and up) all have English names, but none of them is American. Replay and Diesel are made in Italy. And Big Star is from France.

English has become the second language of the world. If you are going to develop a brand name for use on the worldwide market, the name had better work in English. It doesn't have to be an English word, but it should sound like one.

On the other hand, care should be taken when translating English slogans into other languages. Sometimes the results can be disastrous. For example: "Come alive with the Pepsi generation," translated into Chinese, comes out as "Pepsi brings your ancestors back from the grave."

The Perdue slogan, "It takes a strong man to make a tender chicken," translated into Spanish means: "It takes an aroused man to make a chicken affectionate." And the Coors beer tag line, "Turn it loose," in Spanish becomes "Suffer from diarrhea."

While we encourage one global message for a brand, sometimes changes must be made to accommodate languages other than English.

BMW has been the ultimate driving machine for twenty-five years. What's even more remarkable is the fact that BMW retained its strategy even though the brand was driven through three separate advertising agencies. A change of agencies usually signals the end of a brand's consistency.

19

The Law of Consistency

*A brand is not built overnight. Success is
measured in decades, not years.*

The law which is violated most frequently is the law of
consistency.

A brand cannot get into the mind unless it stands for
something. But once a brand occupies a position in the
mind, the manufacturer often thinks of reasons to change.

"The market is changing," cries the manufacturer,
"change the brand."

Markets may change, but brands shouldn't. Ever. They
may be bent slightly or given a new slant, but their essential characteristics (once those characteristics are firmly
planted in the mind) should never be changed.

If the market swings another way, you have a choice.
Follow the fad and destroy the brand. Or hang in there
and hope the merry-go-round comes your way again. In
our experience, hanging in there is your best approach.

Tanqueray is the leading high-end gin. But Absolut and Stolichnaya have created a trend toward high-end vodka. So Tanqueray introduces Tanqueray vodka.

Will Tanqueray vodka cut into the Absolut market? Of course not.

Will Tanqueray vodka undermine the Tanqueray gin market? Ultimately, yes.

Tanqueray should stick with gin and hope the market swings in this direction.

Brands are used as personality statements. (Some marketing people call these statements "badges.") Your choice of a badge is often determined by the statement you want to make to friends, neighbors, co-workers, or relatives. Sometimes it is determined by the statement you want to make to yourself. "I drive a BMW."

As people grow up, they often want to change their personality statements. When kids grow up, they inevitably want to make a statement about their newfound maturity by changing brands . . . from Coca-Cola to Budweiser, for example. If Coca-Cola decided to try to retain these customers by "moving with the market," it would then logically introduce a product called Coca-Cola beer.

As stupid as Coca-Cola beer might seem to you, conceptually it's no different from Tanqueray vodka, Coors water, or Crystal Pepsi. Markets may change, but brands should stay the same.

In the liquor business, bourbon and whiskey are known as brown goods and gin and vodka as white goods. There may be a trend from brown to white (and there is), but should Brown-Forman introduce Jack Daniel's vodka? We think not.

Of course it did introduce Jack Daniel's beer and Jack Daniel's coolers. The beer went nowhere and was killed. The coolers continue to hang on, but what does a sissy cooler brand do to Jack Daniel's core image?

There may be a trend to Mexican food (and there is), but should a French restaurant add fajitas to its menu? We think not.

Brand building is boring work. What works best is absolute consistency over an extended period of time. Volvo has been selling safety for thirty-five years. BMW has been the ultimate driving machine for twenty-five years.

When people do boring work, they get bored. So every once in a while, someone at a company like Volvo gets a bright idea. "Why should we limit ourselves to dull, boring, safe sedans? Why don't we branch out into exciting sports cars?"

So Volvo recently launched a line of sports cars and even a convertible. What will a ragtop do for the Volvo brand? Nothing—except dilute the safety message.

Meanwhile, BMW introduces a station wagon version of the ultimate driving machine. "Hey, why limit ourselves to carefree yuppies? We need to have a vehicle for the young urban professionals when they grow up, get married, and have kids." (Have you ever driven a station wagon through the cones on a test track?)

What did the station wagon do for BMW? Nothing, except erode the driving image in the mind of the consumer.

Consistency built the Little Caesars brand and lack of consistency is in the process of destroying the Little Caesars brand.

"Pizza. Pizza," became the chain's rallying cry. Where else could you get two pizzas for the price of one? The power of this branding program made Little Caesars the second-largest pizza chain in America.

"Why should we limit ourselves to take-out pizza only?" the bored executives asked. So Little Caesars introduced "Delivery. Delivery." And promptly fell to third place in sales, after Pizza Hut and Domino's Pizza.

It gets worse. In order to turn the chain around, Little Caesars went big. The small pizza became a medium-size pizza. The medium-size pizza became a large pizza. And the large pizza became an extra-large pizza.

Talk about confusion. "I'd like to order a medium-size pizza, please."

"Do you want a Pizza Hut medium, which is actually our small size? Or do you want a Little Caesars medium, which is actually a Pizza Hut large?"

"Uh . . . do I still get two pizzas for the price of one?"

"Pizza. Pizza? No, we don't do that anymore."

A pity. Little Caesars had one of the best brands in the pizza category. The only brand focused on takeout. The only brand with an identity and a message. (Pizza. Pizza.)

And now it has lost much of its identity. Another victim of the law of consistency.

Actually, many Little Caesars stores are drifting back to the two-for-one strategy that the company should never have abandoned in the first place.

McDonald's has been a kid-oriented family hamburger place for decades. "Why should we limit ourselves to kid-oriented products? Why not introduce an adult hamburger to compete with Burger King and Wendy's?"

So the Arch Deluxe was born. One hundred fifty million dollars' worth of advertising later, the Arch Deluxe is declared a disaster. And McDonald's quietly decides to drop it from the menu.

Notice one thing. It's always the product that is declared a failure, never the branding concept. McDonald's is a kid-oriented, family restaurant. In such a setting, an adult hamburger might taste good in the mouth, but is not going to taste good in the mind.

Run up a red flag whenever you hear the words: "Why should we limit ourselves?"

You should limit your brand. That's the essence of branding. Your brand has to stand for something both simple and narrow in the mind. This limitation is the essential part of the branding process.

Limitation combined with consistency (over decades, not years) is what builds a brand.

Rome wasn't built in a day. Neither is a brand of Romano cheese.

CITIBANK✦

**Citibank is in the process of changing
from a corporate bank to a consumer bank.
It plans to make Citibank the first global
consumer bank. It will take a while, but it can
be done. So far, so good. But now comes the
merger with Travelers Group, which threatens
the entire branding process.**

20

The Law of Change

*Brands can be changed, but only
infrequently and only very carefully.*

Having harped on the idea of consistency and focus,
why would we bring up the concept of change?

Because nothing in life, nothing in branding, is ever
absolute. There are always exceptions to every rule. And
the law of change is the biggest exception to the laws of
branding.

Where does the change occur? Companies are often
focused on what they need to do internally in order to
facilitate the change of a brand. The procedures, the man-
uals, the brochures, the press conferences, the advertising, the marketing.

But brand changing does not occur inside a company. It
occurs inside the mind of the consumer. If you want to
change your brand, keep your sights on your target, the
consumer's mind.

There are three situations where changing your brand is feasible.

Your Brand Is Weak or Nonexistent in the Mind

This is the easiest situation of all. In essence, there is no brand, so you can do anything you want with the brand name. Use it on a totally different product in a totally different category, if you will. Who's to know?

In 1985, Intel made a dramatic decision to get out of D-RAM (dynamic random access memory) chips in order to focus on microprocessors, a product Intel invented. In the process, Intel made its name the best-known worldwide brand of microprocessor. "Intel Inside" became the theme of a brand-building program of exceptional power. (In many cases customers are more concerned with the brand name of the processor than they are with the brand name of the personal computer.)

Intel changed its brand from D-RAMs to microprocessors. But except for a handful of computer executives and purchasing agents, who knew Intel used to stand for D-RAMs?

You Want to Move Your Brand Down the Food Chain

If you are permanently lowering the price of your brand, you can often move it down the price ladder without hurting the brand. Customers will believe they are getting a lot of value by purchasing your brand. It's not necessarily a bad move. Marlboro lowered its cigarette prices and gained market share.

There's a lot of prestige in building Rolls-Royces, but not a lot of profit. Sometimes prices get out of line and permanent adjustments need to be made.

Going in the other direction, moving up the food chain, is much harder if not impossible. Holiday Inn Crowne Plaza was a difficult sell until the chain dropped the Holiday Inn from the name.

Your Brand Is in a Slow-Moving Field and the Change Is Going to Take Place Over an Extended Period of Time

Twenty-five years ago Citicorp (and its Citibank subsidiary) was 80 percent corporate and 20 percent consumer. Today the numbers are almost reversed. Citicorp is 30 percent corporate and 70 percent consumer.

Citicorp is successfully moving its Citibank brand from corporate to consumer business. But the key concept to keep in mind is that little change has actually occurred in the mind of the banking prospect. Instead of "changing" minds, Citicorp has allowed enough time to pass so that the natural process of "forgetting" takes place.

What works in banking just won't work in a fast-moving field like computers or consumer electronics. There's not enough time for the "forgetting" process to take place.

Customers are never wrong. That's one of the many human traits that is so endearing and yet so frustrating from a branding point of view. When you try to tell customers that your brand is different than it used to be, they will reject your message.

- Xerox computers? No, Xerox is a copier.
- IBM copiers? No, IBM is a computer.
- Epson computers? No, Epson is a computer printer.

In a Miller Lite television commercial, the beer drinker sees a famous ex-football player and says, "You're ah . . . you're ah . . . you're ah . . ."

"Nick Buoniconti," says the famous ex-football player helpfully.

"No, that's not it."

Funny and also true. What you think your brand is doesn't really matter. It's only what your customer thinks your brand is that matters.

Kentucky Fried Chicken has been trying to walk away from the "fried" in its name for a long time. First, it changed the name of the chain to "KFC," but that didn't help much because customers think, "What do those initials stand for?" Second, it promoted its rotisserie chicken as the healthier alternative to fried chicken.

Guess what happened? People still went to KFC for fried chicken. Recently, KFC threw in the towel and went back to promoting fried chicken. "We're going to brag about the original recipe," said one franchisee, "the one that brought us to the dance."

You can be sure that the concept that brought your brand to the dance is still firmly embedded in your prospect's mind.

If you want to change your brand, first look into the mind. Where are you? Perhaps you're not in the mind at all. Fine, change away.

But if you are in the mind, and if you have a unique and distinct perception, then change your brand at your own risk. It's going to be a long, difficult, expensive, and perhaps impossible process.

Don't say we didn't warn you.

Film photography is slowly being replaced by digital photography. But Kodak refuses to face that reality. Instead it is trying to save its brand by using the Kodak name on its digital products.

21
The Law of Mortality

No brand will live forever. Euthanasia is often the best solution.

While the laws of branding are immutable, brands themselves are not. They are born, grow up, mature, and eventually will die.

It's sad. Companies are willing to spend millions to save an old brand, yet they resist spending pennies to create a new brand. Once you understand the nature of branding, you'll know when it is time to let your old brand die a natural death.

Opportunities for new brands are constantly being created by the invention of new categories. The rise of the personal computer created opportunities for Compaq, Dell, Gateway, Packard Bell, and other brands.

But the rise of the personal computer also put pressure on minicomputer brands like Digital, Data General, and Wang.

It's like life itself. A new generation appears on the scene and goes off in exciting new directions. Careers are born and blossom. Meanwhile, the old generation withers and dies.

Don't fight it. For brands, like people, there is a time to live and a time to die. There is a time to invest in a brand and there is a time to harvest a brand. And, ultimately, there is a time to put the brand to sleep.

"Tide's in. Dirt's out." The rise of detergent brands like Procter & Gamble's Tide put pressure on laundry soap brands like Rinso and Oxydol, which eventually faded away.

Companies make serious errors of judgment when they fight what should be a natural process. Yet the Nursing Home for Dying Brands does a booming business with millions in advertising and promotional dollars being spent to keep terminally ill brands on life-support systems.

Spend your money on the next generation. Save the money spent to prolong your old brand's life and invest it in a new brand with a future.

Many managers make poor financial decisions because they fail to distinguish between two aspects of a brand's value.

- How well known the brand is.
- What the brand stands for.

A well-known brand that doesn't stand for anything (or stands for something that is obsolete) has no value. A brand that stands for something has value even if the brand is not particularly well known.

You can do something with a brand that stands for something. When you stand for something, you at least have the opportunity to create a powerful brand. This is especially true in the area of publicity.

What's a Kraft? Who knows? When a brand is just well known, but doesn't stand for anything, it doesn't lend itself to publicity and other branding techniques. It has nowhere to go but down.

What's a Kodak? A conventional camera and a conventional photographic film. But that market is slowly shifting to digital photography.

Look what happened to the 8mm motion picture camera and film. For amateurs at least, film cameras are dead. They have been almost totally replaced by electronic systems using videotape. So how did Kodak try to compensate for the loss of the amateur movie film business it used to dominate? Of course. It put its Kodak brand name on videotape cassettes.

Does the Kodak brand dominate the videotape business? Of course not. Kodak stands for photography. The Kodak brand has no power beyond the realm of conventional photography.

But videotape is only a side skirmish to the main battle that is developing between photographic cameras and digital cameras. Long term, Kodak's billion-dollar photographic business is in jeopardy. Will the market go digital?

History is not on Kodak's side. The slide rule has been replaced by the pocket calculator. The analog computer has been replaced by the digital computer. The record album has been replaced by the compact disk. Analog cellular phones are being replaced by digital phones.

In music, television, and telephones, the trend has been toward digital. The average automobile today has more digital computing power than an IBM mainframe had not too many years ago.

Fight or flee? As you might have expected, Kodak has decided to do both. And, in our opinion, Kodak is making major branding mistakes on both sides of the street.

Take the photography side of the street. Kodak has been the major driver in the creation of the Advanced Photo System. Based on a new 24mm film and new electronic control systems, APS gives you a choice of three print formats, plus a lot of other advantages. Besides Kodak's massive up-front investment in APS, the scheme requires photo shops to spend hundreds of millions of dollars for new film-processing equipment.

(You know it spent a lot of money on developing the APS system, because it even gave it a new name, the Kodak Advantix system.)

The question is obvious. Why spend all that money on conventional photography if the market is going digital? Wouldn't it be better to let the old system die a natural death and use the money to build a new digital brand?

Meanwhile, on the digital side of the street, Kodak is

also making a serious error (and this might be its biggest mistake of all). Instead of launching a new brand, Kodak is venturing into the field with the Kodak brand name (Kodak Digital Science).

It will never work. In the first place, there are too many competitors in the market with a digital reputation that Kodak lacks. To name a few: Canon, Minolta, Sharp, Sony, and Casio. Even more important, when a revolutionary new category develops, the inevitable winner is a revolutionary new brand name.

When miniature electronic products became technically feasible, the winning brand was not General Electric, RCA, or Zenith. It was Sony, a brand-new brand.

When videotape rentals of motion pictures became commercially feasible, the winning retail brand was not Sears, 7-Eleven, or any supermarket or drugstore chain. It was Blockbuster Video, a brand-new brand.

When personal computers invaded the office field, the winning brand was not IBM, AT&T, ITT, Hewlett-Packard, Texas Instruments, Digital, Unisys, Motorola, Sony, Hitachi, NEC, Canon, or Sharp. It was Compaq, a brand-new brand.

Whatever happened to Rinso White and Rinso Blue? Almost none of the soap brands survived the detergent era. Will the photography brands do any better in the digital era?

It remains to be seen, but our best guess is no.

VOLVO

Volvo has been selling safety for some thirty-five years. In the process, the brand has become the largest-selling European luxury car. In the past decade, Volvo has sold 849,348 cars in America, ahead of BMW (804,968) and Mercedes-Benz (770,089).

22
The Law of Singularity

*The most important aspect of a brand
is its single-mindedness.*

- What's a Chevrolet? A large, small, cheap, expensive car or truck.
- What's a Miller? A regular, light, draft, cheap, expensive beer.
- What's a Macintosh? A home, office, cheap, expensive personal computer or personal computer operating system.

These are all burned-out brands because they have lost their singularity. They could, of course, remain on the marketing scene for many years because of the line-extension generosity of their competitors. But make no mistake about it. Loss of singularity weakens a brand.

What's an Atari? An Atari used to be a video game, the leading video game as a matter of fact. Then Atari tried to become a computer.

What's an Atari? A brand that has lost its life because it lost its singularity.

It's this singularity that helps a brand perform its most important function in society.

What's a brand? A proper noun that can be used in place of a common word.

- Instead of an imported beer, you can ask for a Heineken.
- Instead of an expensive Swiss watch, you can ask for a Rolex.
- Instead of a thick spaghetti sauce, you can ask for Prego.
- Instead of a safe car, you can ask for a Volvo.
- Instead of a driving machine, you can ask for a BMW.

What's a brand? A singular idea or concept that you own inside the mind of the prospect.

It's as simple and as difficult as that.

Index

Index

Index

Index

HarperCollins Business

The 22 Immutable Laws of Marketing

ALI RIES AND JACK TROUT

Al Ries and Jack Trout, two of the world's most successful marketing strategists, call upon over forty years of marketing expertise to identify the definitive rules that govern the world of marketing.

Combining a wide-ranging historical overview with a keen eye for the future, the authors bring to light 22 superlative tools and innovative techniques for the international marketplace. The authors examine marketing campaigns that have succeeded and others that have failed and why good ideas didn't live up to expectations, and offer their own ideas on what would have worked better. With irreverent but honest insights, and often flying in the face of conventional, but not always successful, wisdom, they give us:

The Law of Candour
be honest with your audience, point out the negatives, and improve your credibility

The Law of Line Extension
don't try to be all things to all people; companies that overextend themselves consistently lose market share

The Law of the Ladder
the battle isn't lost if you fail to be No. 1

The real-life examples, common-sense suggestions and killer instincts contained in *The 22 Immutable Laws of Marketing* are nothing less than rules by which companies will flourish or fail.

0 00 638345 9

Focus

The Future of Your Company Depends On It
AL RIES

Co-author of *The 22 Immutable Laws of Marketing*

IBM had $65 billion in revenues and was still losing money. PepsiCo has almost twice the sales and assets of Coca-Cola, but its stock is worth less than half. What is their problem, shared by hundreds of other businesses worldwide?

Focus has the answer. With practical, no-nonsense advice, Al Ries guides managers back on track and explains why companies that focus on core products and get rid of extraneous, resource-wasting areas are the most successful.

With hard examples from a wide variety of industries, Ries analyses corporations that are focused, and many that are not. He predicts the kind of corporate thinking that is destined to fail, and looks at companies such as Volvo, Blockbuster, Federal Express, Toys 'R' US, American Express and many more.

In today's cut-throat markets, the 'refocusing' issue can make or break a company. This book is vital to chief executives, entrepreneurs, marketing managers and managers of all divisions.

0 00 638735 7

HarperCollins Business

Brand Warriors

Corporate Leaders Share Their Winning Strategies

EDITED BY FIONA GILMORE

Now that consumers are more brand conscious than ever, championing the brand is at the heart of winning business strategies. Nothing is as important if a company is to prosper.

Brand Warriors brings together some of the top brand custodians in the business to talk about the strategies they employ to put their brands in the lead – and keep them there. Seventeen high-profile contributors, including Richard Branson, Frederick W. Smith and Robert Ayling, discuss issues such as the economic value of brands, effective brand architecture, powerful positioning and corporate communications programmes, global marketing and corporate reputation. These highly readable perspectives provide penetrating insights – based upon proven success – that no business leader can afford to ignore.

'Hard to top the brands discussed in this book . . . it offers many stimulating notions about marketing'
Daily Telegraph

0 00 638892 2

HarperCollins Business

The One Minute Sales Person

SPENCER JOHNSON (co author of *The One Minute Manager*)
& LARRY WILSON

The quickest way to more sales with less stress.

For anyone in selling who wants to become a great sales person, and for everyone who ever has to sell an idea or themselves, whatever their career or profession, *The One Minute Sales Person* shows the quickest way to prosper personally and financially.

The phenomenal One Minute methods are based on the fundamental belief that when the customer is satisfied, everyone is satisfied. Discover the secrets of self-management, the integrity of selling 'on purpose' and the wonderful paradox of helping others to get what they want, and you will achieve real and lasting sales success with the least amount of time, effort and stress.

The One Minute Sales Person is the bestseller for bestsellers.

0 00 637015 2

fireandwater
The book lover's website

www.**fire**and**water**.com

The latest news from the book world

Interviews with leading authors

Win great prizes every week

Join in lively discussions

Read exclusive sample chapters

Catalogue & ordering service

www.**fire**and**water**.com
Brought to you by HarperCollins*Publishers*